ESSENTIAL
MALLORCA

 Best places to see 34–55

 Featured sight

Palma 83–104

Tramuntana 123–142

The Northeast 143–156

Original text by Tony Kelly
Updated by Iain Stewart

© Automobile Association Developments Limited 2009
First published 2007
Reprinted 2009. Information verified and updated.

ISBN: 978-0-7495-6014-0

Published by AA Publishing, a trading name of Automobile Association Developments
Limited, whose registered office is Fanum House, Basing View, Basingstoke,
Hampshire RG21 4EA. Registered number 1878835.

Automobile Association Developments Limited retains the copyright in the original
edition © 1999 and in all subsequent editions, reprints and amendments

A CIP catalogue record for this book is available from the British Library

Colour separation: MRM Graphics Ltd
Printed and bound in Italy by Printer Trento S.r.l.

A03616
Maps in this title produced from mapping © KOMPASS GmbH,
A-6063 Rum/Innsbruck

About this book

Symbols are used to denote the following categories:

✚ map reference to maps on cover
✉ address or location
☎ telephone number
🕐 opening times
✋ admission charge
🍴 restaurant or café on premises
  or nearby
Ⓜ nearest underground train station

🚍 nearest bus/tram route
🚉 nearest overground train station
⛴ nearest ferry stop
✈ nearest airport
ℹ tourist information office
❓ other practical information
➤ indicates the page where you will
  find a fuller description

This book is divided into five sections.

The essence of Mallorca pages 6–19
Introduction; Features; Food and Drink;
Short break including the 10 Essentials

Planning pages 20–33
Before you go; Getting there; Getting
around; Being there

Best places to see pages 34–55
The unmissable highlights of any visit
to Mallorca

Best things to do pages 56–79
Good places to have lunch; best
viewpoints; top activities; good beaches;
quiet coves; places to take the children
and more

Exploring pages 80–186
The best places to visit in Mallorca,
organized by area

Maps
All map references are to the maps on
the covers. For example, Alcúdia has the
reference ✚ 8B – indicating the grid
square in which it is to be found.

Admission prices
€ inexpensive (under €3)
€€ moderate (€3–€6.50)
€€€ expensive (over €6.50)

Hotel prices
Price are per room per night: € budget
(under €60); €€ moderate (€60–€120);
€€€ expensive to luxury (over €120).

Restaurant prices
Price for a three-course meal per person
without drinks:
€ budget (under €15);
€€ moderate (€15–€30);
€€€ expensive (over €30).

Contents

BEST THINGS TO DO

56 – 79

EXPLORING...

80 – 186

The essence of...

THE ESSENCE OF MALLORCA

Mallorca's character is shaped, above all, by its climate. The people of the Mediterranean know how to take life slowly – they still have time to sit in the shade and chat, to take a siesta rather than rush back to work, to enjoy the outdoors whether it is the mountains or the sea.

The warm climate has long attracted outsiders, whose influence can still be felt; Romans, Arabs and Europeans have all left their mark on Mallorca's landscape and culture. But what have not changed are the enduring values of an island people, courteous, proud and self-sufficient.

features

Mallorca is changing its image. Fed up with being labelled cheap and cheerful, it has gone for a new approach. High-rise apartment blocks are being torn down, to be replaced by tree-lined promenades. Manor houses and country estates are being converted into stylish hotels. Tourists are encouraged to come in winter, to walk, cycle and play golf. The island that led the way into mass tourism is now leading the way out.

For such a small island, the variations are extraordinary. You can spend one day lying on the beach, the next walking in the mountains. Castles, caves, countryside, hidden coves...whatever you want from a holiday, it is probably there. Except, perhaps, snow.

Of course there is nowhere in Mallorca still waiting to be 'discovered' – even the tiniest villages are heavily dependent on tourism. But strike off the main roads and into the small towns on the plain, or venture into the foothills to explore scenic villages

and pine-forested walking trails, and you will find a Mallorca utterly at odds with the familiar image.

GEOGRAPHY
● Mallorca is the largest of the Balearic Islands, a group that includes Menorca, Ibiza and Formentera.
● Mallorca measures 100km (62 miles) from east to west and 75km (46 miles) from north to south.
● Mallorca lies 200km (125 miles) south of Barcelona, off the east coast of Spain.

- Mallorca has 555km (345 miles) of coastline and 80 beaches.
- The rocky islands Cabrera and Sa Dragonera provide havens for nesting seabirds.
- The two mountain ranges of Serra de Tramuntana and Serra de Llevant are divided by a fertile central plain.
- Palma has an average daily maximum temperature of 21.4°C (70.5°F) and an average of seven hours of sunshine per day all year round.

TOURISM

- Mallorca received 1 million tourists in 1966, 3 million in 1978 and 9.6 million in 2007, of whom 37 per cent were from Germany, 25 per cent from Britain and 18 per cent from Spain.
- On busy days in summer more than 700 flights land at Palma airport, carrying upwards of 100,000 passengers.
- Mallorca has 289,000 hotel beds and 60,000 in tourist apartments.
- Mallorca has enough restaurant tables for a quarter of the population to eat out every night.

LANGUAGE

- The official languages are Catalan and Castilian Spanish, though Catalan has enjoyed a strong revival in recent years and is now the preferred language in education and local government.
- Most people speak Mallorquín, a dialect of Catalan.

PEOPLE

Of some 830,000 inhabitants, almost half live in the capital, Palma. The next biggest towns are Manacor (36,000) and Inca (25,000). The population has doubled since 1950 and includes a large number of expatriates – mostly German and British.

food & drink

Mallorcan cuisine, based on pork, fish and vegetables with generous use of garlic and olive oil, is hearty peasant fare steeped in tradition and rooted in local ingredients.

Not long ago every village would celebrate the *matança*, the winter slaughter of pigs, with songs and dancing and the making of hams and sausages for the coming year. Sausages come in several varieties – *sobrasada* (raw minced pork with hot red pepper) and *botifarró* (cured pork with blood), as well as spicy *chorizo* from Spain. And no bar would be complete without its *jamón serrano*, a whole cured ham displayed on an attractive slicing board.

MALLORCAN SPECIALITIES

A side effect of the *matança* was *frit mallorquí*, a fry-up of the most perishable offal with potatoes, onions and tomatoes. Nowadays you find it on menus alongside *tumbet*, a Mallorcan-style ratatouille of aubergines, potatoes and peppers in olive oil, and *sopes mallorquines*, a thick broth of thinly sliced brown bread and vegetables. Other classic dishes include *llom amb col* (pork wrapped

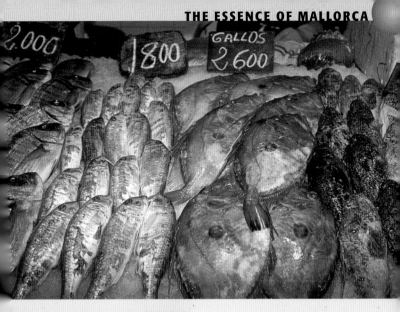

in cabbage with pine nuts and raisins) and *lechona asada* (roast sucking pig).

Paella is not a Mallorcan dish but it is widely available; *paella ciega* (blind man's *paella)* comes without bones. The local equivalent is *arròs brut* ('dirty rice'), saffron rice cooked with chicken, pork and vegetables. Fresh fish is expensive in Mallorca, especially the locally caught John Dory *(gall)*, grouper *(anfós)* and red mullet *(moll roquer)*, but expertly grilled or pan-fried. Salmon, turbot and gilthead *(orada)* are imported. You'll also find prawns, squid and lobster.

Desserts are not Mallorca's strong point – often the choice is between *helado* (ice cream) and *flan* (crème caramel). An interesting alternative is *gato de almendras*, almond cake served with toasted almond ice cream. *Ensaimadas* are fluffy, spiral-shaped pastries dusted with sugar and filled with

anything from pumpkin jam to *sobrasada* sausage; the secret ingredient is the lard in the pastry. Cheeses include Mahón from Menorca, Manchego from central Spain and local varieties.

WINE

The *vi* or *vino de la casa* will probably be Mallorcan, but most bottled wine is imported from the mainland. Some of the best red wines come from La Rioja and Ribo del Duero – wine labelled *crianza* is aged in oak for at least a year, *reserva* for two,

gran reserva for three. Penedés and Cava (sparkling) wines from Catalunya are good value. But don't disparage Mallorcan wines – the best stand comparison with anything at the same cost from mainland Spain. Two well-regarded wineries are Anima Negra and Finca Son Bordils.

OTHER ALCOHOLIC DRINKS

Spanish and imported beer *(cerveza)* are available everywhere – for draught beer, ask for *una caña*. Sherry is always *fino* – dry and chilled. Spanish brandy *(coñac)* comes in a bewildering variety of bottles and is added to coffee at any time of day. Gin is manufactured on Menorca – ask for the Xoriguer brand. Local liqueurs include *hierbas secos* (dry) and *hierbas dulces* (sweet), both based on aniseed and packed full of herbs.

SOFT DRINKS

Tap water is safe but everyone drinks mineral water – *con gas* (sparkling), *sin gas* (still). Fresh squeezed orange juice *(zumo de naranja)* is delicious, as are *granizados* (fruit slushes) of orange or lemon. An unusual local drink is *orxata* or *horchata* – almond milk. *Café solo* is a small shot of strong black coffee; *café con leche* comes with hot milk. If you want something less stimulating, ask for *manzanilla* (camomile) or *poliomenta* (peppermint tea).

short break

If you only have a short time to visit Mallorca, and would like to take home some unforgettable memories you can do something local and capture the real flavour of the island. The following suggestions will give you a wide range of sights and experiences that won't take very long, won't cost very much and will make your visit very special.

● **Spend a day in Palma** exploring the old city, then join the evening *passeig* on the waterfront for a drink in one of the island's trendiest bars (➤ 83–104).

● **Take the joyride to Sóller** on a vintage electric train through the mountains (➤ 134–135).

● **Enjoy a boat trip** around the coast, passing hidden coves which you cannot reach in a car.

● **Walk in the Serra de Tramuntana** (➤ 133),
breathing in the heady mix of fresh air, sea breeze,
pine forests and wild herbs.

● **Sit at a quayside restaurant** eating fresh fish –
choose from any one of the island's ports.

● **Visit the monastery at Valldemossa** (➤ 54–55) where Chopin and George Sand spent the winter of 1838–39.

● **Drive (or walk) to a hilltop sanctuary** to experience 'the other Mallorca' – if you really want to get away from it all, spend the night.

● **Visit the traditional market at Sineu** (➤ 181) to haggle over everything from sausages to sheep.

● **Discover a remote cove beach** – there are dozens of bays scattered around the coastline.

● **Find out where there is a local festival going on** (➤ 24–25) – and drop everything to get there.

Planning

Before you go

WHEN TO GO

JAN	FEB	MAR	APR	MAY	JUN	JUL	AUG	SEP	OCT	NOV	DEC
14°C	15°C	17°C	19°C	22°C	26°C	29°C	29°C	27°C	23°C	18°C	15°C
57°F	59°F	63°F	66°F	72°F	79°F	84°F	84°F	81°F	73°F	64°F	59°F

● High season ● Low season

The above temperatures are the average daily maximum for each month. Minimum temperatures can often be very much lower than this. They may drop to as little as 2 or 3°C (35 or 37°F) during January and February, but they seldom drop below 20°C (68°F) in July and August.

Sunshine is almost guaranteed throughout the summer, which is the peak tourist season. If you want to avoid the crowds come during May, June, September or October.

Many resorts close during the winter, and this may be a good time to take a city break in Palma or a walking or golfing holiday. During winter it may still be warm enough to eat outside, but bring suitable clothes for cool evenings, particularly in the mountains.

WHAT YOU NEED

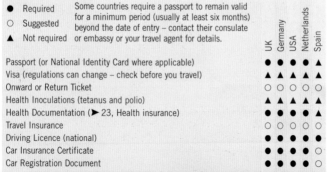

● Required	Some countries require a passport to remain valid for a minimum period (usually at least six months) beyond the date of entry – contact their consulate or embassy or your travel agent for details.	UK	Germany	USA	Netherlands	Spain
○ Suggested						
▲ Not required						
Passport (or National Identity Card where applicable)		●	●	●	●	▲
Visa (regulations can change – check before you travel)		▲	▲	▲	▲	▲
Onward or Return Ticket		○	○	○	○	○
Health Inoculations (tetanus and polio)		▲	▲	▲	▲	▲
Health Documentation (► 23, Health insurance)		●	●	●	●	▲
Travel Insurance		○	○	○	○	○
Driving Licence (national)		●	●	●	●	●
Car Insurance Certificate		●	●	●	●	○
Car Registration Document		●	●	●	●	○

WEBSITES

- www.illesbalears.es (the official tourism portal of the Balearics, with interesting cultural content)
- www.mallorcaonline.com (useful site with plenty of links to everything from diving to rural hotels)
- www.okspain.org (official website for Tourist Office of Spain)
- www.spain.info (official website for Tourism in Spain)
- www.digitalmajorca.com (Mallorca/Majorca tourist information site)

TOURIST OFFICES AT HOME

In the UK
Spanish Tourist Office
✉ PO Box 4009,
London W1A 6NB
☎ 0207 486 8077

In the USA
Tourist Office of Spain ✉ 666 Fifth Avenue 35th Floor, New York, NY 10103 ☎ 212/265-8822

Tourist Office of Spain ✉ 1395 Brickell Avenue, Suite 1130, Miami, FL 33131 ☎ 305/358-1992

HEALTH INSURANCE

Nationals of EU and certain other countries can get medical treatment with the relevant documentation (European Health Insurance Card/EHIC); private medical insurance is still advised and is essential for all other visitors.

Dental treatment is not usually available free. A list of *dentistas* can be found in the yellow pages of the telephone directory. Dental treatment should be covered by private medical insurance.

TIME DIFFERENCES

| GMT | Mallorca | Germany | USA (NY) | Netherlands | Rest of Spain |
| 12 noon | 1PM | 1PM | 7AM | 1PM | 1PM |

Like the rest of Spain, Mallorca is one hour ahead of Greenwich Mean Time (GMT+1), but from late March until late October, summer time (GMT+2) operates. The Spanish attitude to time is much more laid-back than in northern Europe.

NATIONAL HOLIDAYS

1 January *New Year's Day*

6 January *Epiphany*

March/April *Good Friday and Easter Monday*

1 May *Labour Day*

15 August *Assumption of the Virgin*

12 October *National Day*

1 November *All Saints' Day*

6 December *Constitution Day*

8 December *Feast of the Immaculate Conception*

25 December *Christmas Day*

Many shops and offices close for longer periods around Christmas and Easter, as well as for the festivals of Corpus Christi in May/June and Sant Jaume on 25 July

WHAT'S ON WHEN

January *Cabalgata de los Reyes Magos* (5 Jan): The Three Kings arrive by boat in Palma to distribute gifts to the city's children.
Sant Antoni Abat (16–17 Jan): Processions of pets and farm animals in Palma, Artà and Sa Pobla.
Sant Sebastià (19 Jan): Bonfires and barbecues in Palma's squares, and religious processions in Pollença.

February *Sa Rúa* (final weekend before Lent): Carnival held in Palma and elsewhere on the last weekend before Lent. It is marked by bonfires, fancy dress and processions of decorated floats. In Montuïri the Carnival is known as *els darres dies* (the last days).

March/April *Semana Santa* (Holy Week): A week of solemn Easter preparation begins on Palm Sunday, when palm and olive branches are blessed at churches across the island before being taken home to adorn front doors. During Holy Week there are processions every day in Palma, the biggest on Maundy Thursday. Other towns and villages have their own processions too. On the evening of Good Friday a figure of Christ is lowered from his cross in Pollença and carried down the Calvary steps in silence. A similar event takes place on the church steps in Felanitx.

May *Moros i Cristianos* (8–10 May): Mock battles between heroes and infidels in Sóller, commemorating a 1561 battle in which local women helped to defeat a band of Turkish pirates.

June *Sant Pere* (28–29 Jun): Processions of fishing boats in Palma, Port d'Andratx and Port d'Alcúdia in honour of the patron saint of fishermen.

July *La Virgen del Carmen* (16 Jul): Processions of boats in the island's ports, including Cala Rajada, Port de Pollença and Port de Sóller.
Santa Catalina Tomás (27–28 Jul): Homage to Mallorca's patron saint in her home town of Valldemossa.

August *Sant Bartomeu* (24 Aug): Devil-dancing in Montuïri at one of Mallorca's oldest festivals.
Sant Agusti (28 Aug): *Cavallets* dances in Felanitx, with children dressed as cardboard horses being chased by giants to the accompaniment of bagpipes, flutes and drums.

September/October Harvest festivals including a melon festival in Vilafranca de Bonany (second Sun in Sep), a wine fair in Binissalem (last Sun in Sep) and a *botifarró* (blood sausage) festival in Sant Joan (third Sun in Oct).

December *Festa de l'Estendard* (31 Dec): Palma commemorates the anniversary of the Christian conquest with a procession from the town hall to Mass at the cathedral.

Mallorcan festivals
Most traditional *festas* are religious in origin and a few date back to the time of the Christian conquest. Every town and village has its saint's day, whose eve *(revelta)* is marked by a *verbena*, a street party with music, dancing, fireworks and fancy dress. Battles are acted out between devils and heroic women, or Christians and Moors, and people prance about as horses.

Getting there

BY AIR

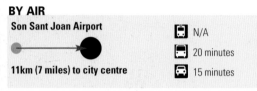

Son Sant Joan Airport

11km (7 miles) to city centre

🚌 N/A

🚆 20 minutes

🚗 15 minutes

Palma's Son Sant Joan Airport (tel: 971 789000/789099; www.aena.es), about 11km (7 miles) east of Palma city centre, is where most people first arrive in Mallorca. It began as a provincial airport and has grown to become one of the busiest in Europe during the peak summer months of June to September, handling more than 23 million passengers each year.

The main terminal is surprisingly spread out and the baggage handling area is quite a way from the flight gates; it can be up to a 30-minute walk from some gates to the baggage area, but there are some moving walkways.

Son Sant Joan has all the amenities of a modern airport, including an information desk and tourist information office on the ground floor. There are plenty of ATMs and a café and newsagent, all on the ground floor, and a post office is situated on the second floor. The pre-departure lounge on the fourth floor has a good range of shops selling wines and spirits, food, jewellery and electronic equipment, as well as a branch of La Caixa bank and a pharmacy.

AIRPORT TRANSFERS

Outside the airport there are plenty of taxis 24 hours a day, but they are expensive. In the arrivals hall of the airport there is a price list of standard journeys around the island where you can check your fare before you take the taxi.

BUSES

The No 1 bus runs from the airport (6:10am–2:15am daily) to Palma via the Plaça d'Espanya and then on along the seafront to the maritime station and port. At the Plaça d'Espanya you can catch trains and other buses for destinations around the island.

ARRIVING BY SEA

Although most visitors fly into Mallorca, over a million arrive by sea on the many cruise ships that ply the Mediterranean waters and the ferries that cross to the island from mainland Spain and the other outlying islands. They dock in Palma harbour, but the car and passsenger ferries from Menorca, Barcelona, Ibiza and Valencia dock at the commercial port at Palma.

From the port you can catch the No 1 bus into Palma, from where you can connect with transport to get around the island.

Getting around

PUBLIC TRANSPORT

Trains The main railway line connects Palma to Inca, with branch lines to Sa Pobla (via Muro) and Manacor (via Sineu and Petra). There are regular trains throughout the day, taking around 35 minutes to Inca and 1 hour to Manacor (tel: 971 752245). Five trains a day leave Palma for Sóller (1 hour), beginning at 8am (tel: 971 752051) and connecting with the tram to Port de Sóller (➤ 130–131). The two railway stations are found close together in Palma, beside Plaça d'Espanya.

Buses A comprehensive network of buses connects Palma to Mallorca's main towns, with extra services linking the coastal resorts in summer. Buses out of Palma depart from the bus station on Carrer Eusebi Estada, behind Plaça d'Espanya. Palma has its own network of city buses, which also covers the beach resorts around Palma Bay (tel: 971 214444). Bus No 1 runs from 6:10am to 2am between the airport, city centre and port.

Boat trips In summer there are regular boat tours of Palma Bay and excursions from resorts including Cala d'Or, Port de Pollença and Port de

Sóller. Some go to remote beaches which can only be reached by boat. There is also the day trip to Illa de Cabrera (► 159). One trip which runs throughout the year is the journey around the northwest coast from Port de Sóller to Sa Colobra (tel: 971 630170).

MENORCA

Day trips to Menorca can be made on a fast catamaran, which leaves Cala Rajada at 9am daily, arriving at the Menorcan city of Ciutadella in one hour. The return journey leaves Ciutadella at 7:30pm (Cape Balear tel: 902 100444). There are also daily car ferries to Ciutadella from Port d'Alcúdia (tel: 902 119128).

TAXIS

Taxis can be hired at ranks (indicated by a blue square with a 'T'), on the street (by flagging down those with a green light) or at hotels. They are good value within Palma but expensive over long distances. A list of tariffs is displayed at taxi ranks.

DRIVING

- Drive on the right.
- Speed limits on motorways *(autopistas)*: 120kph (74mph); dual carriageways: 100kph (62mph); major roads: 90kph (56mph); urban roads: 50kph (31mph)
- Seat belts must be worn at all times. Children under 12 must use a child seat.
- Random breath-testing takes place. Never drive under the influence of alcohol.
- All rental cars take either unleaded petrol *(sin plomo)* or diesel *(gasoleo)*. The top grade is *Super Plus* (98-octane), though *Super* (96-octane) is usually acceptable. Petrol stations are normally open 6am–10pm, and closed Sundays, though larger ones (often self-service) are open 24 hours. Most take credit cards. Note: there are few petrol stations in the mountain areas, so make sure you fill up.

CAR RENTAL

The leading international car rental companies have offices at Palma airport and you can reserve a car in advance (essential in peak periods)

either direct or through a travel agent. Local companies offer competitive rates and will usually deliver a car to the airport.

If the rental car you are driving breaks down follow the instructions given in the documentation; most of the international rental firms provide a rescue service. Note that if you suffer an accident or a breakdown on a dirt road, most insurance policies are invalid.

FARES AND CONCESSIONS

Students Holders of an International Student Identity Card may be able to obtain some concessions on travel, entrance fees etc, but Mallorca is not really geared up for students. However, there are two youth hostels on the island, one near Palma and the other outside Alcúdia, and there's a network of excellent mountain hostels *(refugis)* designed for hikers walking the Tramuntana mountain trails. Another cheap form of accommodation is to stay in a monastery; just turn up or book ahead.

Senior citizens Mallorca is an excellent destination for older travellers, especially in winter when the resorts are quieter, prices more reasonable and many hotels offer very economical long-stay rates. The best deals are available through tour operators who specialize in holidays for senior citizens.

Being there

TOURIST OFFICES
(Oficinas de Información Turística – OIT)

Palma
✉ Plaça de la Reina 2, Palma 07012 ☎ 971 712216
✉ Ca'n Solleric, Passeig des Born 27, Palma 07012 ☎ 971 724090
✉ Plaça d'Espanya, Palma 07002 ☎ 902 102365

Palma Nova
✉ Passeig de la Mar 13, Calvià 07181 ☎ 971 682365

Port d'Alcúdia
✉ Passeig Marítim 68, Alcúdia 07410 ☎ 971 547257

Port de Pollença
✉ Carrer de les Monges 9, Pollença 07470 ☎ 971 865467

Sóller
✉ Plaça d'Espanya, Sóller 07100 ☎ 971 638008

LOCAL TOURIST OFFICES
Other offices include: Cala d'Or, Cala Millor, Cala Rajada, Cala Sant Vicenç, Ca'n Picafort, Colònia de Sant Jordi, Magaluf, Peguera, Platja de Muro, Port de Sóller, Porto Cristo, S'Arenal, Ses Illetes and Santa Ponça.

MONEY
The euro (€) is the official currency of Spain. Notes are in denominations of 5, 10, 20, 50, 100, 200 and 500 euros; coins are in denominations of 1, 2, 5, 10, 20 and 50 cents, and 1 and 2 euros.

TIPS/GRATUITIES

Yes ✓ No ✗		
Restaurants (if service not included)	✓	10%
Cafés/bars (if service not included)	✓	change
Taxis	✓	10%
Porters	✓	€1
Chambermaids	✓	€1
Cloakroom attendants	✓	change
Toilets	✗	

Euro traveller's cheques are widely accepted, as are major credit cards. Credit and debit cards can also be used for withdrawing cash from ATMs.

POSTAL AND INTERNET SERVICES

Post offices are generally open Monday to Friday 9–2, but some also open in the afternoon and on Saturday morning. The main post office in Palma at Carrer de Constitució 5 is open Monday to Friday 8:30am to 8:30pm and Saturday 9–2 (tel: 902 197197). Post boxes are bright yellow.

Internet cafés are fairly widespread in Mallorca, particularly in the resorts. Most towns also have a cybercafé or two, though central Palma is strangely lacking in places where you can surf the net. Increasingly, many bars are offering free WiFi access, though speeds are often slow.

TELEPHONES

Most public telephones accept coins, credit cards and telephone cards *(tarjetas telefónicas)*, available from post offices, news kiosks and tobacconists. Instructions are printed in English.

All telephone numbers in Spain have 9 digits. Telephone numbers in Mallorca begin with 971; you must dial all nine digits wherever you are calling from.

To call Mallorca from the UK dial 00 34; from the USA dial 011 34. To call the operator dial 002.

Using the telephone in your hotel room is considerably more expensive than using a public telephone outside.

Emergency telephone numbers

Police (Policía Local): 092
Police (Policía Nacional): 091
Fire (Bomberos): 080

Ambulance (Ambulància): 061
In any emergency dial 112

International dialling codes

From Mallorca (Spain) to:
UK: 00 44
Germany: 00 49

USA: 00 1
Netherlands: 00 31

EMBASSIES AND CONSULATES

UK ☎ 971 712445
Germany ☎ 971 707737

USA ☎ 971 403707
Netherlands ☎ 971 716493

HEALTH ADVICE

Sun advice The sunniest (and hottest) months are July and August, with an average of 11 hours sun a day and daytime temperatures of 29°C (84°F). During these months particularly you should avoid the midday sun and use a strong sunblock.

Drugs Prescription and non-prescription drugs and medicines are available from pharmacies *(farmàcias)*, distinguished by a large green cross. They are able to dispense many drugs which would be available only on prescription in other countries.

Safe water Tap water is generally safe though it can be heavily chlorinated. Mineral water is cheap to buy and is sold as *con gas* (carbonated) and *sin gas* (still). Drink plenty of water during hot weather.

ELECTRICITY

The power supply in Mallorca is 220–22 volts. Sockets accept two-round-pin-style plugs, so an adaptor is needed for most non-Continental appliances and a transformer for appliances operating on 100–120 volts.

OPENING HOURS

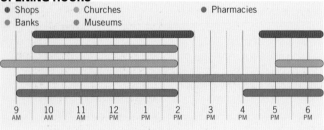

Large department stores, supermarkets and shops in tourist resorts may open outside the times shown above, especially in summer. In general, pharmacies, banks and shops close on Saturday afternoon.

Banks close all day Saturday, June to September, but stay open until 4pm Monday to Thursday, October to May.

The opening times of museums is just a rough guide; some are open longer hours in summer, while hours are reduced in winter. Some museums close at weekends or another day in the week.

LANGUAGE

The language that you hear on the streets is most likely to be Mallorquín, a version of Catalan. Catalan and Spanish both have official status on Mallorca, and though Spanish will get you by (it is still the language used by Mallorcans to address strangers), it is useful to know some Catalan, if only to understand all street signs which are being replaced in Catalan.

yes/no	si/no	how are you?	com va?
please/thank you	per favor/gràcies	do you speak English?	parla anglès?
hello/goodbye	hola/adéu		
good morning	bon dia	I don't understand	no ho entenc
good afternoon	bona tarda	how much?	quant es?
goodnight	bona nit	open/closed	obert/tancat
excuse me	perdoni	today/tomorrow	avui/demà
hotel	hotel	room service	servei d'habitació
bed and breakfast	llit i berenar	bath/shower	bany/dutxa
single room	habitació senzilla	toilet	toaleta
double room	habitació doble	balcony	balcó
one person/night	una persona/nit	key	clau
reservation	reservas	lift	ascensor
bank	banc	banknote/cheque	bitllet de banc/xec
exchange office	oficina de canvi	traveller's cheque	xec de viatge
post office	correus	credit card	carta de crèdit
coin	moneda	exchange rate	tant per cent
café/bar	cafè/celler	main course	segón plat
breakfast	berenar	dessert	postres
lunch/dinner	dinar/sopar	bill	cuenta
starter	primer plat	beer/wine/water	cervesa/vi/aigua
aeroplane/airport	avió/aeroport	single ticket	senzill-a
train/bus	tren/autobús	return ticket	anar i tornar
station/bus stop	estació/la parada	car/petrol	cotxe/gasolina
boat/port	vaixell/port	how do I get to...?	per anar a...?
ticket	bitllet	where is...?	on és...?

Best places to see

1 Alcúdia

A perfectly restored walled city on the site of a Roman settlement, with remains of Roman houses and an amphitheatre.

Not to be confused with the holiday resort of the same name, which is actually at Port d'Alcúdia (➤ 150), the old town is a historic settlement, a maze of narrow streets enclosed by carefully restored medieval ramparts. There were Phoenician and Greek settlements here, but the town reached its heyday in the 2nd century BC, when the Roman invaders made it their capital, Pollentia ('power'). Destroyed by Vandals in the 6th century, the town returned to greatness under the Moors, who built *al-kudia* ('the town on the hill'). The walls you see today were added after the Spanish conquest in the 14th century.

You enter the city through one of the two town gates – the Portal del Moll, with two square towers and two palm trees standing guard, is the symbol of Alcúdia. The narrow streets of the old town, especially Carrer d'en Serra, are resonant of Palma's Arab quarter.

A short walk from the parish church of Sant Jaume takes you to three interesting sights, connected by footpaths. Closest to town are the remains of Roman houses at Pollentia, **Ciutat Romà;** near here are the Teatre Romà (Roman amphitheatre) and the Oratori de Santa Anna, one of Mallorca's oldest churches. After exploring the Roman remains, find out more about them at the **Museu Monogràfic de Pollentia.**

Depending on your appetite for souvenirs and local crafts, you may want to visit (or avoid) Alcúdia on market days.

➕ 8B 🍴 Restaurant Sa Plaça (€€) 🚌 From Palma/Port d'Alcúdia ❓ Market Tue, Sun

Ciutat Romà
🕐 Tue–Fri 10–4, Sat–Sun 10:30–1
✋ Inexpensive

Museu Monogràfic de Pollentia
✉ Carrer Sant Jaume 30 ☎ 971 547004
🕐 Tue–Fri 10–3:30, Sat–Sun 10–12:45
✋ Joint entry with Ciutat Romà

2 Badia de Palma

The good, the bad and the ugly sides of Mallorca's tourist development meet along a 25km (15.5-mile) stretch of coast.

The former villages of S'Arenal and Magaluf sit facing each other across Palma Bay. Once upon a time, a fisherman casting his net into the sea at S'Arenal could have gazed around an empty coastline where the only buildings to stand out

would have been Palma's cathedral and castle.
Nowadays he would barely be able to distinguish
them among a continuous stretch of hotels and
sprawling villa complexes, an urban jungle
extending all the way to Magaluf. And he wouldn't
be there anyway as there are few fish left to catch.

Like it or loathe it, Palma Bay is the engine room
of Mallorca's economy. Each of the resorts
(described separately) has its own character –
young or old, British or German, cheap and
cheerful or jet-set rich. One moment you can be
in Portals Nous, with its chic marina crammed
with millionaires' yachts (you have to be seriously
rich just to look at the restaurant menus here),
the next in seedy Magaluf, all British pubs and wet
T-shirt contests.

Occasionally you come across a glimpse of what
this coastline must once have been like. Follow the
road beyond Magaluf through the pine woods.
Suddenly you are among tiny coves like Cala Mago,
where, out of season, you might still find your own
private beach. Eventually you reach the headland of
Cap de Cala Figuera where you can look back at
sweeping views of the entire bay. Cliffs plunge into
the clear blue sea, with not a hotel in sight. Come
up here at midnight for utter peace and solitude;
but listen carefully and you might just be able to
hear the disco beat of Magaluf pounding away
beneath you.

✚ 16J ⑪ Bars and restaurants in all the resorts (€)
🚍 From Palma to all the resorts 🚢 Boat tours of
Palma Bay in summer from Palma, S'Arenal, Palma Nova
and Magaluf

3 Cap de Formentor

This wild peninsula on Mallorca's northeast tip has stunning views, sandy beaches and the island's original luxury hotel.

The 20km (12.5-mile) drive from Port de Pollença to Mallorca's most northerly point has scenery as dramatic as anyone could wish for. Cliffs 400m (1,310ft) tall jut into the sea, their weird rock formations attracting nesting seabirds, while pine trees seem to grow out of the rocks. The drive is also famously scary – a local legend has it that the parish priest and the local bus driver arrived at the Pearly Gates, and only the driver was admitted to heaven. The reason? He had led far more people to pray.

Six kilometres (4 miles) from Port de Pollença you reach the Mirador des Colomer – scramble up the steps for views over a rocky islet. A path opposite the steps leads to an old watchtower from which you can see the whole of the peninsula as well as the bays of Pollença and Alcúdia. The road continues through pine woods and past more *miradors* (each one helpfully indicated with a picture of an old-fashioned camera) before tunnelling through En Fumat mountain, where you look down over Mallorca's most inaccessible beach. Eventually you reach a lighthouse with the inevitable bar and shop and more stunning views, all the way to Menorca on a good day.

On the way back, stop at Formentor beach and the Hotel Formentor, which opened in 1929 and has been pampering the rich and famous ever since. The fine sandy beach used to be reserved for the hotel's guests, but democracy has opened it to the masses.

✚ 9A 🍴 Cafés with snacks at Cap de Formentor's lighthouse and beach (€); restaurant (€€€) in Hotel Formentor 🚌 From Palma and Port de Pollença in summer 🚢 From Port de Pollença to Formentor beach and Cap de Formentor in summer ❓ The best time to see birds and flowers is spring

4 Castell d'Alaró

A popular walk to a ruined castle and hilltop chapel offering spectacular views all the way to the sea.

A castle has stood on this site since Moorish times; it was so impregnable that the Arab commander was able to hold out for two years after the Christian conquest. Later, in 1285, two heroes of Mallorcan independence, Cabrit and Brassa, defended the castle against Alfonso III of Aragón and were burned alive on a spit when he finally took it by storm. Their punishment was a consequence of their impudent defiance of the king. They pretended to confuse Alfonso's name with that of a local fish – *anfós*, shouting: 'We like our *anfós* grilled.' The present ruins date from the 15th century and seem almost to grow out of the rock, dominating the landscape for miles around.

The climb up here is one of Mallorca's most popular walks, especially on Sundays. From the town of Alaró it is a stiff climb of about two hours, following the signs from the PM210 to Orient; you can also leave from Orient (▶ 128), following a small path opposite L'Hermitage hotel, again taking around two hours in total. The paths converge above Es Verger restaurant (you can even bring a car this far if you don't mind the potholes and the hairpin bends), where you can fill up with roast lamb to fortify you for the final steep climb.

At last you reach the castle, 800m (2,625ft) above sea level; look back at the view, stretching across the entire plain to Palma and out to sea. A few minutes further brings you to the summit, with a small chapel and sanctuary, and (bliss!) a restaurant and bar. If you are inspired by the views, you can stay the night here in one of the simple rooms and experience the true tranquillity of the place.

✚ 5D ☎ Sanctuary: 971 182112 ⚹ Open access
🍽 Es Verger (€€) on the way up; simple restaurant (€) at the sanctuary 🚌 From Palma to Alaró

5 Coves d'Artà

www.cuevasdearta.com

A fascinating network of underground caverns, whose weird stalactites and stalagmites conjure up mysterious images of Heaven and Hell.

If you only have time to visit one set of caves on the east coast, this is the one. Now that they are a sanitised tourist attraction, it is hard to imagine how French geologist Édouard Martel felt when he first

stepped into these caves, dark, mysterious and terrifying, in 1876. In fact they had been known about for centuries – Jaume I found 2,000 Arabs hiding here with their cattle during the Christian conquest and they were later used by hermits, pirates and smugglers – but it was Martel who first studied and chronicled these grottoes, 46m (150ft) above the sea at Cap Vermell, at the instigation of Archduke Ludwig Salvator. Another early visitor was Jules Verne; the caves are said to have inspired his *Journey to the Centre of the Earth*.

The guided tour comes with special effects and the various chambers are given Dantesque names – Hell, Purgatory, Paradise. The descent into Hell is swiftly followed by a *son et lumière* display. Stalactites point down from the mouldy roof like daggers, somehow defying gravity. One of the chambers is as large as the nave of Palma Cathedral, and the Queen of Pillars, a stalagmite 22m (72ft) tall, could almost be a Gothic column. It is growing upwards at the rate of 2cm (0.7in) every 100 years; in another 5,000 years or so it will be joined to the ceiling.

You emerge from the caves to a view of the sea, framed by the cavern entrance. Visitors with limited mobility will find the staircases particularly difficult. All visitors should be sensibly shod.

✚ 12E ☎ 971 841293 🕔 May–Oct daily 10–6; Nov–Apr daily 10–5 ✋ Expensive 🍴 Bars at Platja de Canyamel near by (€) 🚌 From Artà and Cala Rajada in summer

6 Deià

An idyllic village of green-shuttered, ochre-coloured houses has become a millionaires' hideaway in the shadow of the Teix mountain.

Deià could have been just another pretty Mallorcan village had Robert Graves not decided to make it his home. The English poet and novelist first moved here in 1932 with his mistress Laura Riding and returned in 1946 with his second wife. Muses followed, friends came to stay, and before long Deià had established a reputation as a foreign artists' colony. Now it is on every tourist itinerary as the prime example of 'the other Mallorca' and this small village contains two luxury hotels. Rich foreign residents, like the actor Michael Douglas, are apt to bemoan the arrival of tour buses; the few locals who remain are philosophical about outsiders.

Graves was hardly the first to discover Deià. An 1878 guidebook noted its 'collection of strange and eccentric foreigners' and it has stayed that way ever since. Climb the Carrer es Puig, Deià's only real street, passing ceramic Stations of the Cross, to reach the parish church and the small cemetery where Graves is buried. His tombstone, like many others, is inscribed in simple handwriting set into the drying concrete –

Robert Graves, Poeta, 1895–1985.
Graves' house, Ca'n Alluny, which he
helped design and build, has been
converted into a museum dedicated to
the writer (➤ 125).

From Deià you can scramble down
to Cala de Deià, a small shingle beach
set in an attractive cove, where there's
an excellent, if ramshackle, seafood
restaurant (open May–Oct).

✚ 3D 🍴 Abundance of quality restaurants, including
Jaume (€€) 🚌 From Palma, Valldemossa and Port de Sóller
❓ Classical music festival Aug–Sep

7 Es Baluard

www.esbaluard.org

Beautifully designed and exuding real metroplitan style, Palma's stunning new contemporary art museum is a wonderful addition to the city's cutural appeal.

The building itself, occupying a bastion and sections of the city's medieval walls, provides a stunning showcase for the art, with the original fortifications juxtaposed with cutting-edge concrete and glass additions.

Es Baluard has three levels, with the permanent exhibition (much of it donated by local businessman Pere Serra) on the upper two floors, and temporary

exhibitions in the basement. Immediately as you enter, things get off to an interesting start with the aluminium 'needle and neon' sculpture by Ben Jakober and Yannick Vu. Room One has portraits by Picasso, Picabia's haunting *Spanish Lady* and Magritte's *Seduction*, while highlights of the abstract rooms include work by Miró and Borges.

On the upper level there are some early ceramics by Picasso and a vast decked outdoor terrace, plotted with contemporary sculptures by Enrique Salamanca and Rafael Canogar. From the deck, it's possible to walk around the edge of the original fortifications and get a soldier's-eye view of the harbour from one of the watchtowers.

Don't neglect a drink or a meal in the museum's fine café-restaurant, whose terrace has an unmatched perspective of the city. Next to the terrace is *Bou*, a 15m-high (49ft) bronze sculpture by Santiago Calatrava (the Valencian architect of Athens' Olympic stadium), which resembles one of the mobile airport staircases used to get passengers from the runway into the plane – a nice touch in an island so dependent on jet travel and mass tourism.

➕ *Palma 2d* ✉ Plaça Porta Santa Catarina ☎ 971 908200 🕐 Jun–Sep Tue–Sun 10–10; Oct–May Tue–Sun 10–8 🍽 Museum's café-restaurant (€€)

8 Lluc

www.lluc.net

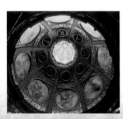

Mallorca's most sacred site – a former monastery in a spectacular setting at the centre of a network of hiking trails in the Serra de Tramuntana.

Lluc has been a centre of pilgrimage since the 13th century when, legend has it, an Arab shepherd boy discovered a dark wooden statue

of the Virgin. The image was put in the local church but three times it returned miraculously to its cave, whereupon the villagers recognized a message from God and built a chapel to house it.

La Moreneta ('the Little Dark One') is now encrusted with precious stones, and sits in a chapel decorated with the arms of every Mallorcan town. Pilgrims and tourists queue to pay homage, especially on Sundays and at 11am before the daily concerts by Els Blauets choir. The choir, named after their blue cassocks, was established in 1531, comprising 40 boys, 'natives of Mallorca, of pure blood, sound in grammar and song'. The service is marred by the whirring and flashing of cameras, and if it's meditation you seek, come back instead for the evening Mass.

The monastery complex includes Els Porxets, the former pilgrims' quarters, and the Way of the Rosary, with touches by Antoni Gaudí. You can stay at Lluc but it is more like a hotel than a hermitage – the 100 'cells' have en suite bathrooms and there are several restaurants and bars. There is also a museum with displays of ceramics, chalices, coins and a collection of paintings by the 20th-century Mallorcan artist Josep Coll Bardolet, with scenes from Deià, Valldemossa and Fornalutx.

✚ 6C ☎ 971 871525 🌐 Museum: daily 10–1:30, 2:30–5. Monastery: daily 9–8:30 ✋ Monastery: free; museum: inexpensive 🍴 Sa Fonda (€€) in the monks' refectory 🚌 Two buses daily from Palma and Inca ❓ Choir concert daily at 11:15 during Mass; second service at dusk open to those staying; annual night-time pilgrimage from Palma to Lluc on foot (48km/30 miles), usually in first week of Aug

9 La Seu (Palma Cathedral)

The glory of Palma – a magnificent Gothic cathedral whose sandstone walls and flying buttresses seem to rise out of the sea.

Anything you see inside Palma Cathedral will come as a disappointment once you have stood on the seafront and gazed up at its golden sandstone exterior, climbing above the old city walls. La Seu stands out from its surroundings, a demonstration of the might of Mallorca's Christian conquerors to all who arrived by sea.

Tradition has it that a storm arose as Jaume I was sailing towards Mallorca. He vowed that if he landed safely he would build a great church in honour of the Virgin. On New Year's Day 1230, a day after the fall of Palma, the foundation stone was symbolically laid on the site of the city's main mosque. Work continued for 400 years – and had to resume in 1851 when an earthquake destroyed the west front. More touches were added in the 20th century by the Catalan architect Antoni Gaudí.

You enter through a side door, passing a small museum; head for the west portal and gaze down the long nave. Light pours in through the rose window, one of the world's largest, 12m (40ft) across and studded with 1,236 pieces of stained glass. The columns are ringed with wrought-iron candelabra by Gaudí; his most controversial addition is the unfinished Crown of Thorns, fashioned from cardboard and cork and suspended above the altar.

Be sure to walk around to the south front, facing the sea, to look at the Portal del Mirador, a 15th-century door by Guillem Sagrera featuring scenes from the Last Supper.

✠ *Palma 5e* ✉ Plaça d'Almoina ☎ 971 723130
🕐 Jun–Sep Mon–Fri 10–6:15, Sat 10–2:15; Apr–May, Oct Mon–Fri 10–5:15, Sat 10–2:15; Nov–Mar Mon–Fri 10–3:15, Sat 10–2:15 ✋ Moderate (free for services) ❓ High Mass Sun 10.30

10 Valldemossa

This small town in the mountains is where Mallorcan tourism began one cold, damp winter in 1838.

Try as it might Valldemossa cannot escape its connection with Frédéric Chopin and his lover George Sand. They arrived in 1838, having rented a former monk's cell, planning to carry on their affair away from the gossip of Paris and hoping that the

climate would benefit Chopin's health (he had TB). Nothing worked out as planned. The weather was wet, the couple were shunned by the locals, Chopin's piano failed to arrive and the relationship never recovered. Sand took out her anger on Valldemossa in a spiteful book, *Winter in Majorca*, labelling the locals as thieves and savages.

The **Reial Cartoixa** (Royal Carthusian Monastery) is the focus of any visit – white-arched corridors lead to 'cells' containing museums on various themes. Visit the old pharmacy, then look into the library, where the monks would meet for half an hour a week, their only human contact. There is a fine modern art museum, with works by Picasso, Miró and Henry Moore.

Most people come for the Chopin experience, but there is more to Valldemossa than that. It is also the birthplace of Catalina Thomás, Mallorca's patron saint. Born in 1531, she became a nun in Palma and was renowned for her humility. Her birthplace at Carrer Rectoría 5 has been turned into a shrine.

Valldemossa's other attraction is Costa Nord (➤ 125–126), established by Michael Douglas.

✚ 3D 🍴 Can Costa, Ctra Valldemossa–Deià (€€) 🚌 From Palma, Deià and Port de Sóller ❓ Regular Chopin piano concerts in Palau del Rei Sanç (entered on same ticket as monastery); La Beata procession in honour of Santa Catalina Thomás, 27–28 Jul; Chopin Festival in Aug; market held Sun

Reial Cartoixa
☎ 971 612106 🕓 Mar–Oct Mon–Sat 9:30–6, Sun 10–1; Nov–Feb, Mon–Sat 9:30–4:30 💰 Expensive

Best things to do

Shopping in Palma

Palma is a vibrant cosmopolitan city with some excellent boutiques, antique and craft shops and specialist food stores. The Passeig des Born area is replete with gorgeous independently owned clothes stores, while there's a huge new shopping mall, the Centro Comercial Porto Pi on Avinguda de Gabriel Roca, about 2km (1.2 miles) southwest of the centre.

Camper
Innovative Mallorca-based shoemaker famous for its hip yet comfy designs.
✉ Avinguda Jaume III 1 ☎ 971 722658

Can Frasquet
A wonderful confectionary shop with a splendid baroque interior and incredible selection of bonbons, *torrons* (nougat), cakes and all things sweet and sticky.
✉ Carrer Orfila 4 ☎ 971 721354

Chocolat Factory
Virtually a museum of chocolate, this superb little place offers 12 different kinds of the dark stuff (from as far afield as Java and Grenada), as well as cakes and desserts.
✉ Plaça d'es Mercat 9 ☎ 971 229493

Drop
Elegant designer clothes, including Frederic Homs and Ikks.
✉ Carrer Josep Tous i Ferrer 2
☎ 971 227409

Joieria Colon 9
One of Palma's foremost jewellers, with some wonderfully crafted silver earrings and necklaces.
✉ Carrer Colon 9 ☎ 971 213838

Marítim
Upmarket shoe store with a range of stylish women's footwear, including the brands Paco Gil and Beverly.
✉ Passeig Maritim 4 ☎ 971 736472

Mola Eyewear
The place on Mallorca for sunglasses, with all the main brands, and some local ones.
✉ Passeig des Born 24 ☎ 971 729236

Good places to have lunch

Aramis (€€€)

Occupying stylish premises inside a historic townhouse, Aramis' lunchtime set menu of flavoursome Spanish, Mallorcan and Italian dishes is great value.

✉ Carrer Montenegro 1, Palma ☎ 971 725232 ✪ Closed Sun

Bens d'Arvall (€€€)

This superb, stylish restaurant has a wonderful terrace ideal for a lunch that extends long into the afternoon. Catalan and Spanish cuisine with strong international inflence.

✉ Deià–Sóller road ☎ 971 632381

Ca'n Antuna (€€)

Dine on Mallorcan cuisine on a terrace overlooking orange groves.

✉ Carrer Arbona Colom 7, Fornalutx ☎ 971 633068 ✪ Closed Mon

Centro (€)

Huge portions, excellent food, ridiculous prices – in an old theatre.

✉ Avinguda Bisbe Campins 13, Porreres ☎ 971 168372 ✪ Closed Sun

Es Verger (€€)

Farmhouse restaurant specializing in roast lamb from a wood-burning oven. Hearty food for hikers.

✉ On the way to Castell d'Alaró ☎ 971 182126

Puig de Sant Miquel (€€)

Roast kid and other Mallorcan specialities beside a hilltop sanctuary near Montuïri.

✉ Carretera de Manacor, km31 ☎ 971 646314 ✪ Closed Mon

Restaurant Es Baluard (€€€)

Perched above Palma's waterfront, this museum restaurant's design is chic and contemporary and the food well-executed Spanish and Mediterranean dishes, with a twist or two. Tables spill out onto a delightful terrace with sublime views of the city walls, marina and over towards La Seu.

✉ Museu Es Baluard, Palma ☎ 971 908199 Ⓢ Closed Mon

Simply Fosh (€€)

This elegant Michelin-starred restaurant, with British chef Marc Fosh at the helm, offers classic French-influenced cooking. The terrace is perfect for a languid lunch, with views across the gardens up to the mountains. There's also a less expensive bistro.

✉ Read's Hotel, Santa María del Camí ☎ 971 140261

Best viewpoints

- Castell d'Alaró (➤ 42–43)

- Castell de Bellver (➤ 86)

- Ermita de Bonany (➤ 166)

- Mirador de Ses Animes, Banyalbufar (➤ 108)

- Mirador de Ses Barques (Sóller–Lluc road)

- Parc de la Mar, Palma (➤ 74)

- Puig de Randa (➤ 176–177)

- Puig de Santa Eugènia (➤ 177)

● Puig de Teix (near Deià)

● Santuari de Sant Salvador (➤ 178–179)

Top activities

Birdwatching: the best areas are the S'Albufera wetlands, the salt flats around Ses Salines, and Gorg Blau and Cúber reservoirs between Sóller and Lluc.

Cycling: bicycle rental is available in resorts. Mountain bikers should pick up a *Guia de Ciclista* (available in English from tourist offices).

Golf: there are more than 20 courses (➤ 72–73).

Horseback riding: several centres have classes for all abilities, including Mallorca Riding School in Bunyola, Carretera de Sóller km12.2, tel: 971 613157.

Sailing: more than 40 marinas. Yachts can be chartered locally and from most marinas. The national sailing school is at Avinguda Joan Miró, Cala Major, tel: 971 402512.

Scuba diving: clubs in Port d'Andratx, Port de Sóller, Palma Nova, Alcúdia and elsewhere (see www.mallorcadive.com).

Swimming: plenty of sandy beaches and sheltered coves. Never go into the sea if the red flag is flying.

Walking: especially in the Serra de Tramuntana. Take a map, compass, sun hat and plenty of water.

Windsurfing: equipment can be rented at most of the main resorts, where there are also schools giving windsurfing lessons.

Good beaches

Quiet coves

- Cala de Deià (➤ 47)

- Cala Pi (south of Llucmajor)

- Cala Santanyí (➤ 160)

- Cala Tuent (➤ 131)

- Portals Vells (➤ 117)

Places to stay

Dalt Murada (€€€)

Highly atmospheric converted town house, where the antiques, chandeliers, beamed ceilings and furnishings are charming. There's a wonderful dining room (where breakfast is served) and a patio area too.

✉ Carrer Almudaina 6A, Palma ☎ 971 425300; www.daltmurada.com

Es Recó de Randa (€€)

This moderately priced rural hotel enjoys a beautiful position at the foot of the Puig de Randa. The pool area is glorious and the restaurant and service is excellent.

✉ Carrer Font 21, Randa ☎ 971 660997; www.esrecoderanda.com

Gran Hotel Son Net (€€€)

Elegantly restored 17th-century mansion with a large swimming pool, set in extensive grounds. Noted for its tasteful décor and fine restaurant.

✉ Carrer Castillo de Sonnet s/n, Puigpunyent ☎ 971 147000; www.sonnet.es

La Reserva Rotana (€€€)

This 17th-century mansion with its own golf course is typical of the new breed of upmarket rural hotels that are opening up in Mallorca.

✉ Camí de S'Avall, km3, Manacor ☎ 971 845685; www.reservarotana.com ✪ Feb–Nov

La Residencia (€€€)

A pair of 16th-century *fincas* with terraced orchards converted into a luxury hotel, considered by many to be the best on the island. There are three pools (one indoor) and a terrific in-house spa with sauna and treatment rooms.

✉ Finca Son Canals, Deià ☎ 971 639011; www.hotel-laresidencia.com
✪ Feb–Nov

Palacio Ca Sa Galesa (€€€)

A beautifully restored 17th-century house between the cathedral and the Arab baths. It has a rooftop terrace and the only indoor pool in the old city.

✉ Carrer de Miramar 8, Palma ☎ 971 715400; www.palacio casagalesa.com

Puro (€€€)

A chic, contemporary, boutique hotel with modish bar and restaurant, where a hip urban crowd laps up the chillout sounds.

✉ Carrer Montenegro 12, Palma ☎ 971 425450; www.purohotel.com

San Lorenzo (€€€)

Nine rooms, some with private patios, in a restored 17th-century manor house, with a rooftop swimming pool and attractive garden, close to the old city.

✉ Carrer Sant Llorenç 14, Palma ☎ 971 728200; www.hotelsanlorenzo.com

Scott's Townhouse Hotel (€€€)

Lavishly decorated 18th-century town house, where the air-conditioned rooms boast ornate covings, high ceilings and fine textiles. In the heart of town, not far from the train station.

✉ Plaça Església 12, Binissalem ☎ 971 870100; www.scottshotel.com

Son Vida (€€€)

Exclusive hotel in a 13th-century castle, with a golf course.

✉ Urbanización Son Vida, Palma ☎ 971 790000; www.hotelsonvida.com

Places to take the children

Aqualand El Arenal

One of the world's largest water funfairs, with enough thrills and spills to keep little ones happy all day.

✉ End of Palma–S'Arenal motorway ☎ 971 440000; www.aqualand.es ⏰ Daily 10–5 🚌 23 from Palma via Platja de Palma

Aqualand Magaluf

There are pools, slides, a 'water castle' and exciting rides at this waterpark on the edge of town.

✉ Carretera Cala Figuera, Magaluf ☎ 971 130811; www.aqualand.es ⏰ May–Oct daily 10–6

Green Park

Reptilarium featuring snakes, crocodiles, tortoises and iguanas in a modern shopping and entertainment complex.

✉ Festival Park, off the Palma–Inca motorway, Marratxi ☎ 971 605481 ⏰ Mon–Fri 10–8, Sat–Sun 10–10

Hidropark

A water-based theme park with activities for very young children, as well as waterslides, wave pools and mini-golf.

✉ Avinguda Tucán, Port d'Alcúdia ☎ 971 891672; www.hidropark.com ⏰ May–Oct daily 10–6

Katmandu

A bizarre-looking haunted house filled with rooms dedicated to themes like 'mysteries of the world', the yeti and mermaids.

✉ Avinguda Pedro Vaquir Ramis 9, Magaluf ☎ 971 134660; www.houseofkatmandu.com ⏰ May–Oct daily 10am–midnight

Natura Parc

An easy walking trail leads around a wildlife park where Mallorcan farm animals can be seen, also butterflies, black vultures and imported species like pelicans and Chinese geese.

✉ Carretera de Sineu, km15, Santa Eugènia ☎ 971 144078 🕙 Apr–Oct daily 10–7; Nov–Mar daily 10–6

Nemo Submarines

See the flora and fauna beneath the sea on a 2-hour exploration by mini-submarine. Expensive.

✉ Carrer Galéon 2, Magaluf ☎ 971 130244; www.nemosub.com 🕙 Mar–Oct daily

Palma Aquarium

This huge state-of-the-art aquarium has more than 700 species of marine life, from sea horses to hammerhead sharks. It's well organized, with excellent educational opportunities. There's also a jungle zone and a good café-restaurant.

✉ Carrer Manuela de los Herreros i Sora 21, Platja de Palma ☎ 971 264275; www.palmaaquarium.com 🕙 Daily 10–6

Western Park

Wild West theme park with cowboy and high-diving shows, thrilling water rides, playgrounds, fast food and video arcades.

✉ Carretera Cala Figuera, Magaluf ☎ 971 131203; www.westernpark.com 🕙 May–Oct daily 10–6

Golf courses

BUNYOLA
Son Termens
Attractive course on an old hunting estate in the Serra de Tramuntana.

✉ Carrer de S'Esglaieta, km10 ☎ 971 617862; www.golfsontermens.com

CALA MILLOR
Son Servera
Nine-hole course amid pine woods by the sea.

✉ Urbanización Costa dels Pins, 6km (4 miles) from Cala Millor ☎ 971 840096

CAMP DE MAR
Golf de Andratx
A challenging course with narrow fairways, lakes and sea views.

✉ Carretera Camp de Mar ☎ 971 236280; www.golfdeandratx.com

CAPDEPERA
Canyamel
A testing course with small greens and sloping fairways.

✉ Urbanización Canyamel ☎ 971 841313

Pula Golf
Challenging course on a luxury golf resort between Capdepera and Cala Millor.

✉ Carretera Son Servera–Capdepera, km3 ☎ 971 817034; www.pulagolf.com

LLUCMAJOR
Son Antem Este
Wide fairways, fast greens and hidden water hazards. There is now a second course, Son Antem Oeste, which is more challenging.

✉ 3km (2 miles) outside Llucmajor on the PM602 to Palma ☎ 971 129200

PALMA
Golf Son Gual
Opened in 2006 to
the north of Palma
and featuring 18
holes set around a
series of lakes.

✉ Finca Son Gual
☎ 971 791532;
www.son-gual.com

Son Vida
Mallorca's first golf course opened in
1964 on an exclusive estate above Palma.

✉ Urbanización Son Vida ☎ 971 791210; www.sonvidagolf.com

POLLENÇA
Pollensa
A tight nine-hole course, with small greens and narrow fairways. If
you're golf's not going too well, the views from the hill out to sea
will make up for it.

✉ 2km (1.2 miles) outside Pollença on Palma road ☎ 971 533216

PORT D'ALCÚDIA
Alcanada
A stunning setting on the Victòria peninsula, overlooking the bay
of Alcudia.

✉ Carretera del Faro ☎ 971 549560

SANTA PONÇA
Santa Ponça
The venue for the Balearic Open, this 18-hole, par-72 course has
long, wide fairways, with some holes set around a lake.

✉ Urbanización Golf Santa Ponça ☎ 971 232531

a walk by the sea

This walk along Palma's waterfront is good in the early morning, as the city stirs itself and the fish market comes to life, or late in the day as the sun sets over the sea, the pavement bars begin to buzz and the cathedral and castle light up for the night.

Start at Parc de la Mar, gazing across at the cathedral reflected in an artificial lake. Cross Avinguda d'Antoni Maura to reach Passeig de Sagrera.

This short tree-lined avenue, named after the architect of La Llotja, passes several interesting buildings. First, La

Llotja itself (➤ 90), Palma's masterpiece of Gothic civic architecture; Porta Vella del Moll, the old gateway to the city from the sea; and finally Consolat del Mar, the former maritime court which houses the Balearic government.

At the end of Passeig de Sagrera, cross the main road to reach the fishing port, marked by lines of blue nets.

West of here, in a small garden, is the oratory of Sant Elm, designed as a navigators' chapel, later used as a tavern, and moved here stone by stone.

From here the walk is straightforward – just follow the seafront west along Passeig Marítim, using the promenade between the road and the sea. A cycle path, also used by joggers, runs alongside the promenade.

Pass Reial Club Nautic, facing a section of city wall and a row of windmills; look up ahead to see Bellver Castle on its hill. As you walk on, turn around to look back at the cathedral, seen across the bay through a forest of masts. From a jetty opposite the Auditorium theatre, excursion boats offer tours of Palma Bay. Keep going, and eventually you reach the marina with its luxury yachts. Just beyond here is the commercial ferry port, where boats leave for Barcelona, Valencia, Menorca and Ibiza.

Return the same way, or take bus 1 back to Passeig de Sagrera.

Distance 3km (2 miles) one way
Time 1.5 hours
Start point Parc de la Mar ✚ *Palma 5a*
End point Club de Mar marina 🚌 1
Lunch Taberna de la Boveda (€€) ✉ Passeig Sagrera 3
☎ 971 720026

Markets

PALMA
Llotja del Peix (Fish Market)
Get here early as the night's catch goes on sale and mullet, prawns, sardines and sea bass are hawked by women with operatic voices.

✉ Es Moll de Pescadors 🕓 Mon–Sat 6am

Mercat Artesanal
Lively craft market on the Plaça Major, with buskers and open-air cafés.

✉ Plaça Major 🕓 Mon–Sat 10–8 in summer; Fri, Sat only in winter

Mercat Olivar
Palma's main market, in a hall near Plaça d'Espanya. Meat, fish and fresh produce on the ground floor, and a supermarket upstairs (➤ 90–91).

✉ Plaça Olivar ☎ 971 720315
🕓 Mon–Sat 8–2

Pere Garau
Local farmers bring their produce – including live animals – to this lively market east of the city.

✉ Plaça Pere Garau 🕓 Mon–Sat 7–2

Rambla
It may not match its Barcelona namesake, but Palma's Rambla is similarly lined with flower stalls.

✉ Passeig de la Rambla
🕓 Mon–Fri 8–2, 5–8

Rastro (flea market)

A Palma institution which takes over part of the main ring road each Saturday morning. Plenty of bargains but lots of junk too.

✉ Avinguda de Gabriel Alomar i Villalonga 🕐 Sat 8–2

Santa Catalina

Fresh fruit and vegetable market just west of the city centre, in the district of the same name. This is where some of Palma's top chefs come to do their shopping. As well as fresh produce, meat and fish, the market also has delicatesen stalls specializing in traditional produce, wine, oils, vinegars and sushi.

✉ Plaça Navegació 🕐 Mon–Sat 7–2

Sineu

Go early to the Wednesday market in the church square at Sineu (➤ 181) to see the best of the fresh produce and the beautiful flower stalls. By mid-morning you will have to fight the crowds as the tour buses bring in more people before the market closes at around midday.

✉ Sa Plaça 🕐 Wed 8–noon

Arts and crafts

ALGAIDA
Ca'n Gordiola
Glass factory and museum (➤ 158) in a mock castle near Algaida.
✉ Carretera Palma–Manacor, km19 ☎ 971 665046; www.gordiola.com

INCA
Munper
Mallorcan leather is rarely a bargain these days, but this is the place to go for a wide selection of shoes, handbags, jackets and coats.
✉ Carretera Palma–Alcúdia, km30 ☎ 971 881000; www.munper.com

MANACOR
OlivArt
Emporium where everything is made from olive wood.
✉ Carretera Palma–Manacor, km45 ☎ 971 552800

PALMA
La Casa del Olivo
Wonderful olive-carver's workshop in an alley off Carrer Jaume II. The best buy here is salad bowls – they're not cheap but you're paying for old-fashioned craftsmanship.
✉ Carrer Pescatería Vella 4 ☎ 971 727025

Herreros de Vicente Juan Ribas
The best place to buy *roba de llengues*, patterned cloth made on the island for over a century. There is another *roba de llengues* shop, Juncosa, in the same street.
✉ Carrer Sant Nicolau 10 ☎ 971 721773

S'Avarca
Traditional Menorcan handmade sandals.
✉ Carrer Sant Domingo 14 ☎ 971 712058

Vidros Gordiola

Exquisite glassware, from a family-owned business that's been around since 1719.

✉ Carrer Victoria 2 ☎ 971 711541

PÒRTOL
Ca Madò Bet

The lovely handmade *siurells* (clay whistles painted white with flashes of red and green) are produced in a village house.

✉ Carrer Jaume I 10, Sa Cabaneta ☎ 971 602156

SANTA MARÍA DEL CAMÍ
Ca'n Bernat

Master craftsman's workshop turning out imaginative local pottery.

✉ Carrer Bartomeu Pasqual ☎ 971 621306

SÓLLER
Toni de Sa Coma

Fine local antiques, including furniture, silver and jewellery

✉ Carrer Vicari Pastor 9 ☎ 971 872418

Exploring

Each region of Mallorca has its own particular appeal – Palma for its thriving arts scene and lively café society, the northeast for history, the east coast for beaches and caves, the north and west for spectacular mountains and picture-postcard villages. And you haven't seen Mallorca until you have driven across *es pla*, the fertile plain at the centre of the island, with its almond groves, windmills and old market towns.

Try to do a bit of everything – one monastery, one mountain walk, one quiet cove – but don't try to do too much. The twisting mountain roads get very crowded in summer and journeys take longer than you think. Take your time and avoid the worst of the heat by doing what the Mallorcans do, break for a siesta. It is generally far more rewarding to spend a day pottering around one small area than to hare from one town to another ticking off the sights.

Palma

Palma de
Mallorca

**Known to the Arabs as Medina Mayurqa
and to Mallorcans simply as _Ciutat_
(City), Palma is in fact named after the
Roman city of Palmaria. Here you can almost literally
uncover the different layers of Mallorcan history. The
Roman city still exists, a metre or two beneath the
ground; inhabitants of houses near the cathedral are
still discovering Roman remains. The cathedral was
built on the site of a mosque, once a Roman temple;
the royal palace replaced an Arab _alcázar_.**

The city you see today, however, is a relatively recent creation. The
tree-lined promenades of La Rambla and Passeig des Born, home
to florists and newspaper sellers, were built in the 19th century on
a dried-up river bed. The walls which once surrounded the city
were pulled down to create the ring road Las Avingudas, and
Passeig Marítim, the waterfront highway and promenade, was
only reclaimed from the sea in the 1950s.

Most of the main sights are located within the area bounded
by the old walls, especially to the north and east of the cathedral.
Wander along any alley in the ancient Arab quarter, peering
through wrought-iron gates and heavy wooden doors, and you will
be rewarded with glimpses of one magnificent patio after another,
with their stone staircases, galleries and arcades.

But you have not truly seen
Palma until you have surveyed
it from the waterfront, with the
cathedral and Almudaina palace
rising proudly above the
defensive walls of the old city,
their golden sandstone lit up by
the afternoon sun.

✚ 16J

🛈 Tourist information ➤ 30

BANYS ÀRABS

These 10th-century baths are virtually all that remain of the Arab city of Medina Mayurqa. They were probably part of a nobleman's house and are similar to those found in other Islamic cities. The *tepidarium* has a dome in the shape of a half-orange, with 25 round shafts for sunlight, supported by a dozen columns. Notice how each of the columns is different – they were probably salvaged from the ruins of various Roman buildings, an early example of recycling. Hammams were meeting places as well as wash houses, and the courtyard with its cactus, palm and orange trees would have made a pleasant place to cool off after a hot bath.

✚ *Palma 6e* ✉ Carrer Can Serra 7 ☎ 971 721549
🕐 Apr–Nov daily 9–7; Dec–Mar daily 9–6
👋 Inexpensive 🍴 Bar Sa Murada nearby (€)

BASÍLICA DE SANT FRANCESC

The facade of this 13th-century church (remodelled after it was struck by lightning in the 17th century) is typically Mallorcan – a massive, forbidding sandstone wall with a delicately carved portal and a rose window at the centre. You enter through peaceful Gothic cloisters with orange and lemon trees and a well at the centre. Inside the church is the tomb of Ramón Llull (1235–1316), the Catalan mystic who became a hermit following a failed seduction attempt and was later stoned to death after attempting to convert Muslims in Tunisia. His statue can be seen on the Palma seafront; outside the basilica is a statue of another famous Mallorcan missionary, Fray Junípero Serra, who once lived in the monastery here. The streets behind the church, which were once home to jewellers and Jewish traders, are now rather run-down and seedy and best avoided after dark.

✚ *Palma 6d* ✉ Plaça Sant Francesc; www.franciscanostor. org ☎ 971 712695
🕐 Mon–Sat 9:30–12:30, 3:30–6, Sun 9:30–12:30
✋ Inexpensive

CASTELL DE BELLVER

A well-preserved royal fortress with an unusual circular structure, this castle has superb views over Palma Bay and dates back to 1300. For many years it was used as a prison, housing Jaume III's widow and her sons. Today it contains Palma's Museum of Municipal History, with important Talaiotic, Roman and Arab artefacts and ceramics.

🔀 *Palma 1d (off map)*, 16H ✉ Carrer Camilo José Cela Parc Bellver ☎ 971 730657 🕐 Apr–Sep Mon–Sat 8am–8:30pm, Sun 10–7; Oct–Mar Mon–Sat 8–7, Sun 10–5 💲 Moderate; free Sun, when museum is closed 🚌 3, 6 to Plaça Gomila

ES BALUARD

Best places to see, ➤ 48–49.

FUNDACIÓ LA CAIXA

The Gran Hotel was Palma's first luxury hotel when it opened in 1903. Designed by Lluís Domènech i Montaner, it began the craze for *modernista* (art nouveau) architecture in the city. Restored by the Fundació la Caixa and reopened in 1993, it is now an art gallery with changing exhibitions and paintings by Hermen Anglada-Camarasa, founder of the 'Pollença school'. On the ground floor is a bookshop and a stylish café-bar.

🔀 *Palma 5c* ✉ Plaça Weyler 3 ☎ 971 178500 🕐 Tue–Sat 10–9, Sun 10–2 💲 Free 🍴 Café and restaurant (€€)

FUNDACIÓ PILAR I JOAN MIRÓ

Painter and sculptor Joan Miró spent most of his life in Barcelona, but both his wife and mother were Mallorcan and he always longed to return to the scene of his childhood holidays to draw inspiration from what he called 'the light of Mallorca'. In 1956, aged 63, he bought a house and studio in Cala Major. He lived here until he died in 1983, after which it was enlarged to hold a permanent exhibition of his works.

The collection includes more than 100 paintings, 25 sculptures and 3,000 studio pieces, but only a small amount is displayed at any time. The paintings are almost childish, all vivid splashes of bright primary colours, influenced by his love of peasant traditions and his fascination with *siurells* (clay whistles). Anyone tempted to remark that their child could do better should take a look at the heavily realistic work that Miró was producing aged eight – the fantasy came later.

✚ *Palma 1d (off map)*, 16H 📩 Carror Joan de Saridakis 29, Cala Major
☎ 971 701420 🕐 16 May–15 Sep Tue–Sat 10–7, Sun 10–3; 16 Sep–15 May Tue–Sat 10–6, Sun 10–3 🖐 Moderate 🍴 Café (€) 🚌 6 from Palma

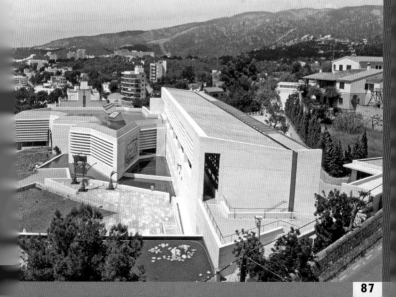

a walk around Palma

Start on Plaça d'Espanya by the statue of Jaume I the Conqueror on horseback. With the station behind you, bear left across the square towards Mercat Olivar (▶ 90–91).

Leave via Plaça Olivar and turn left into Carrer Sant Miquel.

Soon you reach Plaça Major, with its outdoor cafés and street entertainers.

Continue across the square; fork right into Carrer Jaume II.

At the end of this pedestrian shopping street, don't fail to look up at the Moorish-style *modernista* facade of Can Corbella before turning left into Plaça Cort. Beyond a gnarled olive tree you see the town hall.

Take the short street to the left of the town hall to reach Plaça Santa Eulàlia; cross this square diagonally and take Carrer Morey.

This brings you into the heart of the old city. Take your time here admiring the courtyards; don't miss Casa Oleza at No 9.

Continue straight on to Carrer Miramar and turn right onto the city walls.

The cathedral (▶ 52–53) is above you; to visit it and the palace, climb the steps to a large wooden cross.

Back on the walls, continue until you drop to the S'Hort del Rei gardens (▶ 92). Cross Plaça Reina and walk up Passeig des Born (▶ 95), turning right by Bar Bosch into Carrer Unió.

Look out for the old Gran Hotel (▶ 86) on your left and the bakery opposite, two good examples of *modernista* style. Beyond the theatre, the road bends left and becomes La Rambla; stroll up this promenade among the flower stalls.

At the top of La Rambla, turn right into Carrer Oms and follow it back to Plaça d'Espanya.

Distance 3.5km (2 miles)
Time 2 hours; with coffee, browsing and visits – probably half a day

Start/end point Plaça d'Espanya ✚ *Palma 7a*
🚌 Most city buses terminate here; island buses terminate at the nearby bus station on Carrer Eusebi Estada 🚆 Trains from Inca and Sóller also terminate here
Lunch Fundació la Caixa (€) ✉ Plaça Weyler 3
☎ 971 728077

LA LLOTJA

With twin turrets and an angel over the door, this 15th-century seafront building looks half-castle, half-church. In fact it is neither. It was designed by Guillem Sagrera (the architect of the cathedral's Portal del Mirador) as the city's exchange. Stand among the spiralling pillars, gaze up at the rib vaulting, and try to imagine the merchants of 500 years ago haggling over silk, spices and silver. Nowadays La Llotja is a cultural centre, hosting some excellent exhibitions.

✚ *Palma 3d* ☎ 971 711705 ✉ Plaça Llotja ◎ Exhibitions only: Tue–Sat 11–2, 5–7, Sun 11–2 ✋ Free 🍴 Wide choice of restaurants and bars nearby (€–€€)

MERCAT OLIVAR

When you're tired of museums and churches and want to meet the people of Palma instead, head for this large covered market near Plaça d'Espanya. After renovation, there is now a supermarket on the first floor and the ground-floor stalls have been spruced up, but the market has lost none of its atmosphere. Huge piles of oranges and tomatoes, buckets full of olives, meat and cheese counters and fresh fish stalls in a separate annexe all add up to a visual feast. There are also several traditional *tapas* bars, where the market workers can still be seen drinking brandy with their breakfast coffee.

➕ *Palma 7b* ✉ Plaça Olivar ☎ 971 720315 🕐 Mon–Sat 8–2 ✋ Free
🍴 Several *tapas* bars (€) upstairs

MUSEU D'ART ESPANYOL CONTEMPORANI

The private collection of Mallorcan banker Joan March (1880–1962) has been expanded into this small museum of 20th-century Spanish art close to Plaça Major. Among the artists represented are Picasso, Joan Miró and Salvador Dalí, Catalan abstract artist Antoni Tàpies and Cubist artist Juan Gris. A room is dedicated to Miquel Barceló, the avant-garde painter born in Mallorca in 1957.

➕ *Palma 6c* ✉ Carrer Sant Miquel 11 ☎ 971 713515;
www.march.es/arte/palma 🕐 Mon–Fri 10–6:30, Sat 10:30–2 ✋ Free

MUSEU DE MALLORCA

Mallorca's most important museum is housed in a 17th-century palace, with collections spanning more than 3,000 years of history. Start in the basement with the prehistory section, which includes pottery, metal and stone artefacts from the Talaiotic cultures, as well as bronze figures of naked warriors brought back from the Punic wars. Other rooms are devoted to Islamic archaeology, Gothic art, Modernista curiosities, Modernism and 20th-century art.

🚩 *Palma 6e* 🖂 Carrer Portella 5 ☎ 971 717540 ⏲ Tue–Sat 10–7, Sun 10–2 ✋ Inexpensive 🍽 Bar Sa Murada (€) at foot of Carrer Portella

PALAU DE L'ALMUDAINA

A royal palace has stood on this site since the Muslim *walis* (governors) built their *alcázar* soon after the Arab conquest. It was converted into Gothic style, but elements of Islamic architecture remain – like the Moorish arches seen from the seafront, lit up at night like a row of lanterns. The courtyard, flanked by palm trees, is at its best in late afternoon when the sun falls on the cathedral towers overhead. Just off the courtyard is the royal chapel, Capella de Santa Ana.

The S'Hort del Rei gardens below the palace make a pleasant place to sit beneath the fountains watching the world go by. Look out for the Arc de la Drassana, once the gateway to the royal docks; near here is a statue of a *hondero* or Balearic slinger. The gardens were rebuilt in the 1960s, forcing the demolition of several houses; their best-known landmark is Joan Miró's *Egg* sculpture, which few can resist sticking their heads through.

🚩 *Palma 4e* 🖂 Carrer Palau Reial ☎ 971 214134 ⏲ Palace: Apr–Sep Mon–Fri 10–7, Sat 10–2; Oct–Mar Mon–Fri 10–2, 4–6, Sat 10–2. Gardens: open access ✋ Palace: moderate; gardens: free

PALAU MARCH

This quirky museum reflects the eclectic tastes of entrepreneur Joan March and his son Bartolomé. Most striking is the sculpture terrace, in an open courtyard surrounded by an attractive loggia in the shadow of the cathedral. Among the artists represented are Rodin, Henry Moore, Barbara Hepworth and contemporary Spanish sculptors. Highlights include Neapolitan crib figures, 16th-century Mallorcan maps and the original 1940s murals for the Music Room by Josep Maria Sert, with acrobats and carnival scenes.

✛ *Palma 4d* ✉ Carrer Palau Reial 18 ☎ 971 711122; www.fundbmarch. es 🕓 Apr–Oct Mon–Fri 10–6:30; Nov–Mar Mon–Fri 10–5, Sat 10–2

✋ Moderate

🍴 Cappuccino Palau March (€)

PASSEIG DES BORN

For more than a century this short, tree-lined promenade
has been at the heart of city life; it has witnessed *festas*,
demonstrations and countless generations of families
enjoying an evening stroll. Come here to feel the pulse of
Palma from a seat at a pavement café – Bar Bosch, near
the top of the Born in Plaça Rei Joan Carles I, is the
traditional place. Near here is **Ca'n Solleric**, a modern art
gallery in a converted mansion that also houses the city's
tourist office.

✚ *Palma 4d* 🍴 Choice of restaurants and cafés nearby, including
Lizarrán (➤ 99)

Ca'n Solleric

✉ Passeig des Born 27 ☎ 971 722092 🕐 Tue–Sat 10–2, 5–9,
Sun 10–1:30 ✋ Free

POBLE ESPANYOL (SPANISH VILLAGE)

Spain gets the theme-park treatment at this 'village' in the outskirts of Palma, where reproductions of famous buildings from Córdoba, Toledo and Madrid are gathered together with typical houses from the Spanish regions. You can eat Spanish food in the Plaza Mayor (Spanish spellings here) or sit outside a café watching the tourists buy pearls and souvenirs at the village shops. A visit here gives you a whistle-stop tour of Spanish architecture, showing its development through Muslim and then Christian influences. If you have never been to Granada, it's worth coming just for the reproduction of the salon, baths and patio from the Alhambra Palace. Various artists give displays of handicrafts in workshops scattered throughout the 'village'.

🕂 *Palma 1d (off map)* ✉ Carrer Poble Espanyol 39 ☎ 971 737075; www.congress-palace-palma.com ⏰ Daily 9–6; shops closed Sat afternoon and Sun 🍴 Restaurant and cafés (€€) 🚌 5 👋 Moderate ❓ Craft displays from 10am to one hour before closing time

LA SEU (PALMA CATHEDRAL)

Best places to see, ➤ 52–53.

HOTELS

Born (€€)
The hotel, set in a converted mansion in an excellent old town location, has real character. There's a great courtyard, partially shaded by palms, where breakfast is served.

✉ Carrer Sant Jaume 3 ☎ 971 712942; www.hotelborn.com

Ciutat Jardí (€€€)
The Moorish-style building is behind the beach, with fabulous views of Palma, a one-hour walk around the bay.

✉ Carrer Illa de Malta 14, Ciutat Jardí ☎ 971 260007; www.hciutatj.com

Convent de la Missió (€€€)
Fabulous hotel occupying a former seminary, that now boasts cutting-edge minimalist design, a celebrated restaurant, art gallery and fine spa. It's arguably Palma's hippest and most prestigious place to stay.

✉ Carrer Missió 7 ☎ 971 227347; www.conventdelamissio.com

Dalt Murada (€€)
Just eight elegant rooms furnished with antiques in a restored Gothic manor house near the cathedral.

✉ Carrer Almudaina 6A ☎ 971 425300; www.hoteldaltmurada.com

Gran Meliá Victoria (€€€)
A huge modern hotel that dominates the harbour area.

✉ Avinguda Joan Miró 21 ☎ 971 732542; www.solmelia.com

Hostal Brondo (€)
Just behind the famous Bar Bosch, on a quiet street in the historic centre, this British-owned place has classy, comfortable, high-ceilinged rooms decorated with antiques.

✉ Carrer Brondo 1 ☎ 971 719043; www.hostalbrondo.net

Palacio Ca Sa Galesa (€€€)
See page 69.

Portixol (€€€)
Scandinavian design meets 1950s architecture at this seaside hotel in an up-and-coming harbour district.

✉ Carrer Sirena 27 ☎ 971 271800; www.portixol.com

Puro (€€€)
See page 69.

San Lorenzo (€€€)
See page 69.

Son Vida (€€€)
See page 69.

RESTAURANTS

Aramis (€€€)
See page 60.

La Bodeguilla (€€)
Modern variations of classic Spanish cuisine; the same owners have a stylish *tapas* bar next door.

✉ Carrer Sant Jaume 1 and 3 ☎ 971 718274 ⊕ Mon–Sat 1–11.30

Ca'n Carlos (€€)
One of the few restaurants in central Palma to focus on traditional Mallorcan cuisine, including hearty stews and *arròs negre* (rice dish similar to *paella* made with squid ink).

✉ Carrer de l'Aigua 5 ☎ 971 713869 ⊕ Lunch, dinner; closed Sun

Candela (€€€)
In a street better known for its *tapas* bars, this place offers fresh fish and creative Mediterranean cuisine.

✉ Carrer dels Apuntadors 14 ☎ 971 724428 ⊕ Dinner; closed Wed

Ca'n Eduardo (€€)
Traditional fish restaurant above the fish market.

✉ Travessia Pesquera 4 ☎ 971 721182 ⊕ Lunch, dinner; closed Sun

Ca'n Joan de S'Aigo (€)

Classy traditional café where Joan Miró used to go for hot chocolate, almond ice cream and *ensaimadas* (spiral-shaped pastries).

✉ Carrer Sant Sanç 10; Barò Santa Maria del Sepulcre 5 ☎ 971 710759
🕐 Closed Tue

Chopin (€€€)

Top-notch Swiss-Mediterranean dishes on a garden terrace in the back streets close to the Born.

✉ Carrer Ca'n Puigdorfila 2 ☎ 971 723556 🕐 Lunch Mon–Fri, dinner Mon–Sat

Darsena (€€)

Stylish, popular waterfront place that caters for the local yachting community, with food and service from breakfast till late.

✉ Passeig Marítim ☎ 971 180504 🕐 Daily 8am–1am

Fábrica 23 (€€)

One of the hottest restaurants in town is run by an English chef in the Santa Catalina district. Go early if you want a lunchtime table.

✉ Carrer Fábrica 23 ☎ 971 453125 🕐 Lunch, dinner, Tue–Sat

Fundació la Caixa (€€)

Cocktails, cakes, sandwiches and serious meals in the bar of the former Gran Hotel. Very elegant indeed.

✉ Plaça Weyler 3 ☎ 971 728077 🕐 Lunch, dinner; closed Sun dinner

Koldo Royo (€€€)

High-class Basque and Mallorcan contemporary cuisine on the waterfront, with windows overlooking the bay.

✉ Passeig Marítim 3 ☎ 971 732435 🕐 Lunch Tue–Fri, dinner Tue–Sun

Lizarrán (€)

Large, bustling and casual tapas bar strong on atmosphere and low on prices.

✉ Carrer Brondo 6 ☎ 971 721819 🕐 Lunch, dinner daily

La Lubina (€€)
On the quay – try *lubina en sal*, sea bass baked in rock salt.
✉ Es Moll Vell ☎ 971 723350 🕐 Lunch, dinner daily

Mangiafuoco (€€)
Acclaimed Italian restaurant in Santa Catalina, specializing in northern Italian (especially Tuscan) cuisine.
✉ Plaça Vapor 4 ☎ 971 451072 🕐 Lunch, dinner; closed Tue

Na Bauçana (€)
Friendly vegetarian restaurant with set-price midweek lunch.
✉ Carrer Santa Bàrbara 4 ☎ 971 721886 🕐 Lunch Mon–Fri

Opio (€€)
Funky 'Mediterrasian' fusion food at an ethnic-style boutique hotel.
✉ Carrer Montenegro 12 ☎ 971 425450 🕐 Lunch, dinner; closed Mon

El Pilon (€€)
Atmospheric little *tapas* bar in an alley off the Born.
✉ Carrer Ca'n Cifre 3 ☎ 971 717590 🕐 Lunch, dinner; closed Sun

Port Pesquer (€)
Stylish café with superb harbourfront terrace and a long menu, with everything from tapas to fresh fish and lobster.
✉ Avinguda Gabriel Roca ☎ 971 715220 🕐 Lunch, dinner daily

Restaurant Es Baluard (€€€)
See page 60–61.

Sa Cranca (€€)
Come here for proper paella, and Catalan and Balearic rice dishes such as *arròs negre* (black rice).
✉ Passeig Marítim 13 ☎ 971 737447 🕐 Lunch daily

Sa Llimona (€)
Create your own *pa amb oli* with a huge choice of toppings.
✉ Carrer Fábrica 27A ☎ 971 736096 🕐 Dinner daily

Taberna de la Bóveda (€€)

Great *tapas* on a terrace facing the harbour. The original La Bóveda is just around the corner at Carrer Boteria 3. Roasted mushrooms; red peppers and much more.

✉ Passeig Sagrera 3 ☎ 971 720026 🕙 Lunch, dinner Mon–Sat

Taberna del Caracol (€€)

Tapas restaurant in an old stone house close to the Arab Baths.

✉ Carrer Sant Alonso 2 ☎ 971 714908 🕙 Lunch, dinner Mon–Sat

Txakoli (€€)

Charcoal-grilled meat is the speciality at this busy Basque joint in the heart of Santa Catalina.

✉ Carrer Fábrica 14 ☎ 971 282126 🕙 Lunch Mon–Fri, dinner Mon–Sat

SHOPPING

BOOKS

La Casa del Mapa

Books and maps about Mallorca.

✉ Carrer Sant Domingo 11 ☎ 971 225944

Fiol

Palma's leading second-hand bookshop.

✉ Carrer Oms 45 ☎ 971 721428

Fundació la Caixa

Art books and posters in the shop of this modern art gallery.

✉ Plaça Weyler 3 ☎ 971 728071 🕙 Mon–Sat 10–9, Sun 10–2

Ripoll

Antiquarian books and prints.

✉ Carrer Sant Miquel 12 ☎ 971 721355

DEPARTMENT STORE

El Corte Inglés

Branches of Spain's leading department store. The Club del Gourmet has Spanish wines, hams and cheeses.

✉ Avinguda Jaume III 15; Avinguda Alexandre Rosselló 12 ☎ 971 770177
🕐 Mon–Sat 9:30–9:30

FOOD AND WINE
Bon Vins
Excellent selection of Mallorcan and Spanish wines and olive oils.
✉ Carrer Sant Feliu 7 ☎ 971 214041

Can Frasquet
See page 58.

Chocolate Factory
See page 58.

Colmado Santo Domingo
Sobrasada sausages, cheeses, fig cakes, olive oil and more.
✉ Carrer Sant Domingo 1 ☎ 971 714887

Forn d'es Teatre
Art nouveau shopfront and the place to buy *ensaimadas*.
✉ Plaça Weyler 9 ☎ 971 715254

Fosh Food
Gourmet deli with a wonderful selection of cheeses, hams, wine and much more. A lot is from the island, though produce as exotic as Kobe beef is stocked.
✉ Carrer Blanquerna 6 ☎ 971 290108

La Montaña
Sausages, hams, cheeses and one of Palma's best window displays.
✉ Carrer Jaume II 27 ☎ 971 712595

Son Vivot
Mallorcan and Menorcan produce, including *sobrasada*, cheese and wine.
✉ Plaça Porta Pintada 1 ☎ 971 720748

ENTERTAINMENT

BARS

Abaco

Palma's most celebrated bar – in a 17th-century palace close to
La Llotja. Inside, the historic premises are adorned with fresh,
exotic flowers and the atmosphere is convivial.

✉ Carrer Sant Joan 1 ☎ 971 715974 ⏰ 8pm–3am

Atlantico

Popular American-themed old-town bar.

✉ Carrer Sant Feliu 12 ☎ 971 728986 ⏰ 8pm–3am

Bosch

With a large terrace on the fringes of Carrer Born, this place –
popular with artists and writers – serves up decent tapas and
ice-cold beers.

✉ Plaça Joan Carles I ☎ 971 721131 ⏰ 8am–1:30am

Cappuccino Grand Café

The original Cappuccino Grand Café, on the waterfront, is still a
popular place to meet for coffee or late-night cocktails.

✉ Passeig Marítim 1 ☎ 971 282162 ⏰ 8:30am–3am

Dàrsena

Fashionable waterfront terrace bar. Great location.

✉ Passeig Marítim ☎ 971 180504 ⏰ Mon–Sat 8am– midnight, Sun
8am–9pm

Hogans

Palma's first Irish pub opened in 1996. Occasional Irish fiddling.

✉ Carrer Monsenyor Palmer 2 ☎ 971 289664 ⏰ Noon–3am

Varadero

Trendy terrace bar at the end of the old quay, with great views of
the cathedral when it is floodlit at night.

✉ Moll Vell ☎ 971 726428 ⏰ 9am–late

THEATRES AND CONCERTS

Auditòrium
Palma's main venue for theatre and concerts.
✉ Passeig Marítim 18 ☎ 971 734735

Castell de Bellver
Outdoor classical concerts on summer evenings.
✉ Parc Bellver ☎ 971 730657

Parc de la Mar
Free outdoor concerts (jazz, rock or classical) beneath the city walls in summer.
✉ Parc de la Mar

Teatre Municipal
Contemporary drama, dance, ballet and films.
✉ Passeig Mallorca 9 ☎ 971 739148

Teatre Xesc Forteza
Contemporary drama and music.
✉ Plaça Prevere Miquel Maura 1 ☎ 971 720135

SPORTS

FOOTBALL
Son Moix
The home of Real Mallorca FC, who alternate between the top two divisions. Matches are played on alternate Sunday afternoons between September and June.
✉ Camí dels Reis ☎ 971 221221; www.rcdmallorca.es 🚍 No 8

HORSE-RACING
Hipódromo Son Pardo
Trotting races (carreras) are held around a 1km (0.5-mile) track at 4:30pm on Sundays in winter and 9pm on Friday evenings in summer.
✉ Carretera Palma–Sóller, km3 ☎ 971 754031

West of Palma

The west side of Mallorca has examples of all the geographical features and characteristics to be found on the rest of the island, including beautiful beaches, busy resorts, and a more rugged northern coastline as well as some fine mountain scenery. Parts of the coastline were overdeveloped for tourism years ago, but new building is far more regulated and sympathetic to the environment and some of the ugliest hotels have been replaced by palm-fringed promenades.

□ Andratx

The Bay of Palma is popular still with millionaires and nearby Cala Major is the summer home of King Juan Carlos and Queen Sofía of Spain. The marina at Puerto Portals is filled with the yachts of the rich and famous, and celebrities such as racing driver Michael Schumacher and supermodel Claudia Schiffer have holiday homes at chic Camp de Mar.

However, the hinterland has remained unspoiled and here you can still find traditional Mallorcan villages, such as Puigpunyent, where time goes at the most gentle of paces and you feel as though you really have 'got away from it all'.

ANDRATX

Like many towns around the coast, Andratx was built some way inland from its port to deter pirate raids. These days the town is reaping an unexpected benefit – tourists pour into the port, spending money which the town collects in taxes, except on market day when Andratx sees little of the visitors and its people are left to get on with their lives. Surrounded by orange groves and almond trees, Andratx is a sleepy town which only really gets animated on Wednesdays when the streets are taken over by traders selling vegetables, cheeses and fish. When you have finished your shopping, climb to the top of the town to see the 13th-century church of Santa Maria.

✚ 14H 🍴 Bars and cafés (€) 🚌 Regular buses from Palma, Peguera and Port d'Andratx ❓ Market held Wed

BANYALBUFAR

People come to Banyalbufar to see one thing – its terraced hillsides irrigated by a network of gushing water channels, sloping down to the sea. Developed by the Moors and divided by drystone walls, these terraces speak powerfully of man's ingenuity in creating farmland from inhospitable, steep terrain. Until recently it was the custom for each generation to add a further tier. In Moorish times the town, whose Arabic name means 'vineyard by the sea', was famed for its Malvasia wine – nowadays the terraces are mostly used to grow vegetables, though a few vines have been planted again.

Banyalbufar's popularity with foreign artists has led some people to conclude that it will be the next Deià (➤ 46–47).

🕂 2D 🍴 Restaurant Es Trast (€, ➤ 121)

🚌 Bus from Palma

a drive around the West

This drive gives an excellent introduction to the mountain and coastal scenery of western Mallorca.

Start in Andratx, taking the C710 to Estellencs about halfway up the main street.

Immediately the road begins to climb through pine woods and tunnels, with occasional glimpses of the sea. Follow this beautiful twisting coast road to the village of Estellencs, one of the prettiest in Mallorca, with narrow, steep cobbled streets and women doing their washing at the village well. After another 5km (3 miles), stop at the Mirador de Ses Animes and clamber up to the 16th-century watchtower for views right along the northwest coast. Soon after this you reach Banyalbufar (➤ 106–107), with its spectacular terracing.

When the C710 turns off left towards Valldemossa, keep straight on the PM110, signposted to Palma. After 1km (0.5 miles) you see a sign to La Granja on your right.

You could easily spend 2 to 3 hours at this display of Mallorcan traditions (➤ 112).

Leaving La Granja, take the narrow road to Puigpunyent from the car park.

Follow this road for 10km (6 miles), a dramatic journey through olive groves in the shadow of Puig de Galatzó. The road continues through Puigpunyent and on to Galilea (➤ 111), a mountain village with a couple of *tapas* bars and views out to sea. From here the road twists and turns down to the village of Es Capdellà.

Turn right in the village and follow signs back to Andratx.

Distance 62km (38 miles)
Time 3 hours plus lunch and time at La Granja
Start/end point Andratx ✚ 14H
Lunch La Granja (€) ☎ 971 610032

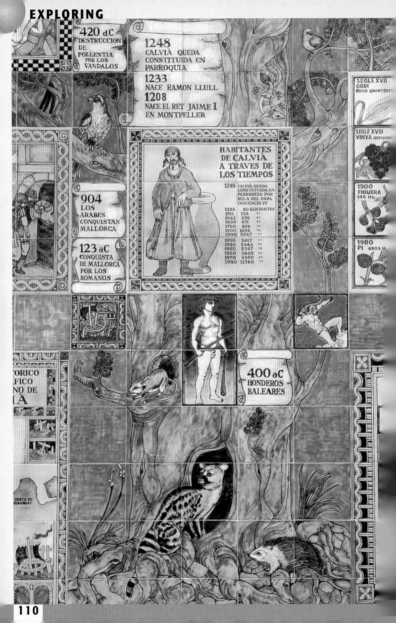

420 dC DESTRUCCION DE POLLENTIA POR LOS VANDALOS

1248 CALVIÀ QUEDA CONSTITUIDA EN PARROQUIA

1233 NACE RAMON LLULL

1208 NACE EL REY JAIME I EN MONTPELLER

SEGLE XVII ORDI 6500 QUARTERES

SEGLE XVIII VINYA 400 QUAR

1900 FIGUERA 144 Ha.

1900 PI 6903 H

904 LOS ARABES CONQUISTAN MALLORCA

123 aC CONQUISTA DE MALLORCA POR LOS ROMANOS

HABITANTES DE CALVIÀ A TRAVES DE LOS TIEMPOS

1248	CALVIÀ QUEDA CONSTITUIDA EN PARROQUIA POR BULA DEL PAPA INOCENCIO IV	
1285	80 HABITANTES	
1511	128	"
1543	296	"
1600	491	"
1700	856	"
1800	1656	"
1900	2567	"
1930	2617	"
1940	2663	"
1950	2327	"
1960	3005	"
1970	4590	"
1980	11560	"

...ORICO ...FICO ...NO DE ...A

400 aC HONDEROS BALEARES

COSTA DE BENDINAT

CALVIÀ

Until recently an unassuming country town, Calvià hit the jackpot when tourists discovered the nearby beaches and it is now said to be the richest municipality in Spain. There are a few ostentatious signs of wealth, like the sparkling new town hall and sports stadium, but mostly life continues as before, with ochre-coloured sandstone houses, fields of gnarled olive trees and a handful of shops and bars. The town is dominated by the church of Sant Joan Baptista, built in the late 19th century around the 13th-century original; near here, by a fountain, a ceramic mural tells the story of Calvià's history. Founded in 1249 with 80 inhabitants, the town had a population of 3,000 in 1960 and 11,560 in 1980 – all because of tourism. Stand on the terrace looking out over almond and carob trees and it is hard to believe you are just a few kilometres from the teeming resorts of 'Maganova'.

✚ 15H ▮▮ Restaurants and bars (€€) 🚌 From Palma ❓ Market on Mon

GALILEA

This pretty village, 460m (1,510ft) above sea level, in the shadow of the great peak of Puig de Galatzó, gets crowded out by day trippers who come to sample the spectacular views from the church terrace. On a good day you can see far out to sea, while eating *tapas* outside the church and listening to the echo of sheep-bells on the hillsides.

The nearby village of Puigpunyent is also justifiably popular and is surrounded by orange groves – as well as being the base for visiting La Reserva (➤ 118).

✚ 2E ▮▮ Two bars (€)

LA GRANJA

This country house, looking out over a glorious wooded valley just south of Banyalbufar, is one of Mallorca's most impressive residences. When Jaume I conquered Mallorca he divided the island into four feudal estates, giving one to Count Nuno Sanç, who settled at La Granja. In 1239, the Count handed the estate to Cistercian monks to found Mallorca's first monastery. Since 1447 it has been a private house; most of what you see today dates from the 17th century.

Highlights of the tour include an aristocratic drawing-room with its own theatre, the family chapel and imposing dining room – but the real reason for visiting is to learn about rural Mallorcan traditions. Workshops, cellars and kitchens contain displays of everyday objects. On Wednesday and Friday afternoons in summer, women in traditional costume give demonstrations of lacemaking, embroidery and spinning, donkeys turn threshing-wheels and there are tastings of cheese, wine, sausages, doughnuts and fig cake. There are also displays of bagpipe music and folk dancing.

Escape from the tour groups by walking in the grounds, which contain botanical gardens, waterfalls and a thousand-year-old yew – there is a 1.2km (0.7-mile) signed walk. La Granja is still a working farm and you may see pigs, turkeys, chickens and goats, as well as displays of agricultural implements and tools.

The restaurant serves good Mallorcan staples like *pa amb oli* and *sopes mallorquines* (thick broth of bread and vegetables).

www.lagranja.net

⊞ 2E ✉ Carrer Esporles Puigpunyent, km2 Esporles ☎ 971 610032 ◉ Apr–Sep daily 10–7; Oct–Mar daily 10–6 ♿ Expensive 🍴 Restaurant (€) 🚌 From Palma ❓ Folk fiesta, Wed, Fri 3:30–5

MAGALUF

More than anywhere else in Mallorca, Magaluf has been blighted by the curse of mass tourism. During the 1980s it became a byword for all that was wrong with Mallorca; foreign TV crews would flock here to film drinking competitions, wet T-shirt contests and teenagers throwing up on the beach. However, in the 1990s Magaluf tried hard to change its image. High-rise hotels have been demolished, a

new seafront promenade has been built, and the council has introduced activities from guided walks to *tai chi* on the beach. But still the lager louts come...and if you want cheap sun, sea, sand and *sangría*, there's no better place.

➕ 15J 🍴 Bars and restaurants (€) 🚌 Regular buses from Palma

PALMA NOVA

There are still people who can remember when this was just a village; then along came the tourist boom, and 'new Palma' became the favoured resort of the British. More restrained than Magaluf and less exclusive than Portals Nous, Palma Nova occupies a prime position on the western side of the bay of Palma. It makes a good base for a family holiday, with nearby attractions including Aqualand Magaluf (➤ 70) – as long as you enjoy sharing your family holiday with a myriad others.

➕ 15J 🍴 Wide choice of restaurants (€–€€) 🚌 Regular buses from Palma

PEGUERA

This beach resort, popular with German tour operators, was the first in Mallorca to have its own artificial beach. Once on the main road from Palma to Andratx, it has become much more peaceful since the construction of a bypass and the opening of a seafront promenade. Just outside Peguera is Cala Fornells, a chic resort of terracotta houses set around a pretty cove. Nearby Camp de Mar is a fast-growing resort where racing driver Michael Schumacher and model Claudia Schiffer both have homes.

➕ 14H 🍴 Wide choice of restaurants (€–€€)
🚌 From Palma

PORT D'ANDRATX

Dress up to come here, or you will feel seriously out of place. Port d'Andratx is one of Mallorca's classiest resorts, popular with the yachting fraternity and with film stars whose Italian-style villas can be seen climbing up the hillsides. Development has increased, but the old town still retains real charm and character. And the harbour is one of the prettiest in Mallorca – a table at one of the waterside bars really is the perfect place to watch the sunset.

➕ 14H 🍴 Wide choice of restaurants (€€–€€€) 🚌 From Andratx

PORTALS NOUS

This is one of the more exclusive resorts in the bay of Palma – not many high-rise hotels here, just rows of private villas and apartments dominating the shoreline. Puerto Portals marina, opened in 1987, is the summer home of the jet set. King Juan Carlos has been known to moor here while staying at his summer palace, Marivent, in nearby Cala Major, and the younger royals can be seen frequenting the waterfront restaurants and bars. Don't even think about looking in the smart boutiques unless you have a high credit card limit.

➕ 16H 🍴 Wide choice of bars and restaurants (€€–€€€) 🚌 From Palma

PORTALS VELLS

A bumpy track from Magaluf leads through pine woods to this beautiful cove at the southwest tip of Palma Bay. In summer it gets crowded, but out of season you could have your own private beach, with golden sand, rocky cliffs and shimmering turquoise water. In fact there are two beaches; the smaller one, El Mago, is Mallorca's official nudist beach. From the main beach, hike along the cliffs to the Cove de la Mare de Déu, a rock chapel built by fishermen. Back on the road, another 2km (1.2 miles) brings you to the headland of Cap de Cala Figuera, topped by a lighthouse, with sweeping views of the entire bay of Palma.

🔢 15J 🍴 Beach bar and restaurant (€€) 🚌 From Palma Oct–May Mon–Fri
☎ 971 717190

LA RESERVA

On the slopes of Puig de Galatzó near the village of Puigpunyent, this nature reserve describes itself as 'Mallorca's paradise'. A 3km

(2-mile) trail of waymarked paths leads you through Mallorca's mountain scenery in less than two hours, past waterfalls and springs, olive trees and charcoal stoves. A series of boards provides information on wildlife and mountain industries. Well laid out and interesting, the reserve gives you a feeling for the area. It will seem a bit sterile if you have been out in the mountains on your own, but it may help you make sense of what you have already seen.

🚩 12E ☎ 971 616622 🕓 Apr–Oct daily 10–7; Nov–Mar daily 10–6 ✋ Expensive 🍴 Café (€)

SA DRAGONERA

This uninhabited island, about 1km (0.5 miles) off Mallorca's western tip, was the focus for a turning point in Mallorcan history in 1977, when it was occupied by environmentalists protesting against a planned tourist development. The campaigners won, the island became a nature reserve instead and for the first time the authorities realized that mass tourism had reached its limit.

Crowned by an ancient watchtower, 6km-long (4-mile) Sa Dragonera takes its name from its shape, said to resemble a dragon. It is rich in birdlife, and the very rare Eleonora's falcon can sometimes be seen here. You can visit in summer by boat from Sant Elm; in winter you have to make do with views from the beach at Sant Elm or from the climb to Sa Trapa (➤ opposite).

🚩 13H 🚢 Mar–Oct from Sant Elm ☎ 639 617545

SANT ELM

The main reason for visiting Sant Elm, a small laid-back resort with a fine sandy beach, is for the views of Sa Dragonera (▶ opposite). You can take a boat to the island from the jetty at the end of the main street, or sit outside the fish restaurants on the same jetty.

A challenging walk from Sant Elm leads to the abandoned

Trappist monastery of Sa Trapa. Set out on Avinguda de la Trapa and climb through coastal *maquis* and pine, with fine views of Sa Dragonera. The round trip takes about 3 hours; a longer route is signposted beside the cemetery on the Sant Elm to Andratx road. Near here is the village of S'Arracó, built by Spanish settlers returning from the American colonies.

✚ 13H 🍴 Choice of restaurants (€€) 🚌 From Andratx or Peguera 🚢 From Port d'Andratx and Peguera in summer

SANTA PONÇA

Santa Ponça's appearance, with its rows and rows of neat modern villas and manicured gardens, belies its place in Mallorcan history. It was here that Jaume I landed in 1229 to begin his conquest of Mallorca, a conquest he described as 'the best thing man has done for a hundred years past'. A relief on a large cross above the marina, erected in 1929, records the event.

✚ 14J 🍴 Bars and restaurants (€–€€) 🚌 From Palma ❓ Rei en Jaume regatta in Jul

SES ILLETES

This genteel resort, with its white villas and old-fashioned hotels, is for many people the most attractive in the whole Badia de Palma. Two small beaches look out over a pair of *illetes* (islets), the larger one crowned by an old watchtower. Its proximity to Palma means that you will never be alone here; in summer the buses from Palma to Ses Illetes are packed out at weekends. But if you want a base near the capital, combining a city break with a beach holiday, this could be just the place.

✚ 16H 🍴 Cafés and restaurants (€€) 🚌 From Palma

HOTELS

BANYALBUFAR
Mar i Vent (€€)
Small, family-owned hotel with attractive rooms and commanding aspects over the Mediterranean.
✉ Carrer Major 49 ☎ 971 618000; www.hotelmarivent.com 🕔 Feb–Nov

PORT D'ANDRATX
Catalina Vera (€)
Modest, hospitable place with comfortable, well-scrubbed rooms a block from the seafront.
✉ Carrer Isaac Peral 63 ☎ 971 671918 🕔 Mar–Nov

SES ILLETES
Bon Sol (€€€)
Delightful family-run hotel, arranged like a wedding-cake on several levels and cascading down a hill, with its own private beach.
✉ Passeig Illetes 30 ☎ 971 402111 🕔 Closed Nov

RESTAURANTS

BANYALBUFAR
Restaurant Es Trast (€)
A welcoming place with a great set menu, tapas and substantial Spanish and Mediterranean dishes. There's a lovely little rear patio.
✉ Carrer Conde Sallent 10 ☎ 971 148544 🕔 Lunch, dinner daily

PALMA NOVA
Ciro's (€€)
Pizzas and other Italian/Mediterranean specialities served on a terrace overlooking the beach.
✉ Passeig del Mar 3 ☎ 971 681052 🕔 Lunch, dinner daily

PORT D'ANDRATX
Rocamar (€€)
This is the place to try Galician and Mallorcan seafood specialities in a perfect terrace setting at the end of the promenade.
✉ Carrer Almirante Riera Alemany 29 ☎ 971 671261 🕔 Lunch, dinner daily

PORTALS NOUS
Tahini (€€€)
This restaurant stands out for its minimalist design and Japanese-inspired fusion food.

✉ Puerto Portals ☎ 971 676025 🕐 Lunch, dinner; closed Mon

SANT ELM
El Pescador (€€)
Fish restaurant on the jetty with its own fishing boat and fine views of Sa Dragonera.

✉ Avinguda Jaume 1 ☎ 971 239198 🕐 Lunch, dinner daily

ENTERTAINMENT

DISCOS AND DINNER SHOWS
BCM
Mega-club with a capacity of 4,000, popular with young Brits. Top British DJs play here in high season.

✉ Avinguda S'Olivera, Magaluf ☎ 971 131546; www.bcm-planetdance.com
🕐 10pm–5am; nightly in summer, weekends in winter

Casino Mallorca
A choice of gambling in the casino (passport and smart dress required) or the Paladium dinner show with dancing.

✉ Urbanización Sol de Mallorca, Magaluf ☎ 971 130000 🕐 Mon–Sat 6pm–4am, Sun 3pm–4am; show Tue, Thu, Fri, Sat 10pm

Pirates Adventure
Yo-ho-ho and a bundle of fun on a mock pirate ship – including acrobatics, comedy and dancing – with lots of audience participation required.

✉ Carretera La Porrassa, Magaluf ☎ 971 130411; www.piratesadventure.com 🕐 May–Oct Mon–Fri (times vary)

Tramuntana

Threading along the northwest coast of the island from Sa Dragonera to Cape Formentor is the Tramuntana mountain range. Many rock-climbers and walkers head to this wild, dramatic landscape that is visible from all over Mallorca. The highest peaks top 1,000m (3,280ft), with Puig Major rising to 1,447m (4,747ft) and unmistakable because of the two white globes of the communications complex that sits atop the peak.

Deià

Tourism is the main source of income in this part of the island and nestled in the mountains are Lluc and Deià, along with luxurious hotels clustered throughout the Serra de Tramuntana. The narrow winding roads become very busy throughout the summer months making the best time to visit the spring and autumn.

CALA SANT VICENÇ

This old-fashioned holiday resort has been given a facelift and is in danger of becoming chic. It is still very popular with Mallorcans, especially on summer weekends. Four small coves, each with its own beach, huddle together beneath Cavall Bernat, a limestone ridge which casts its shadow into the sea. A walk of around 45 minutes leads across the hills to Port de Pollença (➤ 130).

✚ 7B 🍴 Bars and restaurants (€–€€€) 🚌 Bus from Pollença

CA'N ALLUNY

The former home of Robert Graves is now an excellent museum dedicated to the English writer and poet and a mandatory stop if you're in the village of Deià. Visits start with an illuminating short film about the life of Graves, who first moved to Mallorca in 1929, and wrote his most famous work, *I, Claudius*, here at Ca'n Alluny.

Graves designed his own home, all of which is open to the public, and visitors can see his north-facing study, where he wrote with blankets on his lap during the chilly winter months. The upper exhibition room, converted from two former bedrooms and a landing, showcases personal mementoes from Graves's life, while the garden, with its citrus and carob trees, has a wonderful setting above an olive grove.

✚ 3D ✉ Carretera Deià–Sóller km1 ☎ 971 636185; www.fundaciorobertgraves.com ⏰ Daily 10–5 💷 Moderate 🍴 Excellent restaurants in Deià (€€–€€€)

CAP DE FORMENTOR

Best places to see, ➤ 40–41.

CASTELL D'ALARÓ

Best places to see, ➤ 42–43.

COSTA NORD

The American actor Michael Douglas could be seen as a 21st-century successor to Archduke Ludwig Salvator (➤ 136), using his money and his influence to promote the landscapes and culture of Mallorca. In 2000 he opened Costa Nord, a multimedia cultural centre in Valldemossa devoted to

Mallorca's northwest coast. The visit begins with a short film, narrated by Douglas, in which he describes his love for the island; it continues with a recreation of the Archduke's yacht, the *Nixe*, accompanied by a commentary on his Mediterranean voyages. The shop sells a range of pricey souvenirs; there is also a café, a restaurant and a concert hall which attracts top international names during the Mediterranean Nights festival each summer. Costa Nord is a personal tribute to an island which, as Douglas says, has attracted 'poets, painters…and yes, film stars'.

✚ 3D ✉ Avinguda Palma 6, Valldemossa ☎ 971 612425; www.costanord.com 🕐 Apr–Oct daily 10–6; Nov–Mar daily 9–5 💷 Expensive 🍴 Bar and restaurant (€€) 🚌 From Palma and Deià ❓ Mediterranean Nights, Jun–Aug

DEIÀ

Best places to see, ➤ 46–47.

FORNALUTX

Fornalutx, in the hills above Sóller, calls itself the prettiest village in Spain, and it is hard to disagree – unless you accept the claims of its neighbour Biniaraix. There are several terrace restaurants and bars, where you can soak up the sublime views of olive and orange groves climbing up to the pine-clad foothills of Puig Major.

✚ 4C 🍴 C'an Antuna (€€)

JARDINS DE ALFÁBIA

These classical gardens by the entrance to the Sóller tunnel are a legacy of the Arab talent for landscaping and irrigation. Their name derives from *al fabi*, 'jar of olives' in Arabic. They were probably designed by Benihabet, the Muslim governor of Inca who converted to Christianity following the Spanish invasion.

A flight of steps lined with tall palms leads to a covered walkway – from here you can strike off to see lily ponds, bamboo groves or citrus trees growing in the shadow of the mountains.

✚ 4D ✉ Carretera Palma–Sóller, km17 ☎ 971 613123 ☀ Apr–Sep Mon–Sat 9:30–6:30; Oct–Mar Mon–Fri 9:30–5:30, Sat 9:30–1 ✋ Moderate 🍴 Ses Porxeres (€€) in the car park

LLUC

Best places to see, ➤ 50–51.

ORIENT

Nervous drivers should not even think about tackling the 10km (6-mile) hairpin road to Orient from Bunyola (there is a much easier approach from Alaró). But those who make it to this village are rewarded with a marvellous sight – one of Mallorca's tiniest hamlets, with a population of less than 30, nestling among olive trees at the foot of Puig d'Alfábia. Orient is popular with walkers – numerous walks start from here, including an ascent to Castell d'Alaró – and with weekend day trippers from Palma, who visit its three restaurants for Sunday lunch.

✚ 4D 🍴 Three good restaurants (€€)

POLLENÇA

At the eastern end of the Serra de Tramuntana and tucked between two hills, each topped by a sacred site, Pollença is the perfect Mallorcan town. Large enough to avoid being twee but small enough to wander round in a morning, it has none of the feel of other towns which have succumbed to the sheer weight of tourism. Foreigners have long been attracted here, but Pollença has learned to adapt to tourism without losing its identity. Café life is still the rule; if you want to join in, come on a Sunday morning when the Plaça Major is filled with market stalls and the locals congregate after church to relax in the Café Espanyol.

The Pont Romà (Roman bridge) on the edge of town gives a clue to Pollença's long history. The name Pollença dates from the 14th century, when settlers from Alcúdia named the town after their former Roman capital. Among many historic buildings is a former Jesuit convent, now the town hall. From here you climb 365 steps to the Calvari church, with its ancient wooden cross and views of Puig de Maria (▶ 150–151). The steps are the scene of a moving procession each Good Friday, when a figure of Christ is removed from a cross and carried down the steps by torchlight.

The **municipal museum** in the former Dominican convent contains the remains of prehistoric sculptures shaped like bulls, as well as a *mandala* (Tibetan sand painting) given by the Dalai Lama in 1990. The cloisters of the convent are the venue for Pollença's celebrated classical music festival.

➕ 7B 🍴 Excellent cafés and restaurants (€€) 🚌 From Palma ❓ Market held Sun; classical music festival, Jul–Aug; www.festivalpollenca.org; *Devallement* procession, Good Fri; *Moros i Cristians*, mock battle, 2 Aug

Museu de Pollença

✉ Carrer Guillem Cifre de Colonya ☎ 971 531166 🕐 Jul–Sep Tue–Sat 10:30–1, 5:30–8:30, Sun 10–1; Oct–Jun Tue–Sun 10:30–1 🖐 Inexpensive

PORT DE POLLENÇA

This genteel, old-fashioned resort at the mouth of Pollença bay is particularly popular with families, and with older visitors in winter. There is also a large community of foreign residents, mostly retired British. The promenade along Passeig Voramar, all whitewashed villas and pine trees leaning into the sea, is perfect for an early evening walk. Look out for the bust of Hermen Anglada-Camarasa, the Catalan painter who spent many years in Pollença and whose work is displayed in the Fundació la Caixa in Palma (➤ 86). A favourite walk from Port de Pollença is the 3km (2-mile) hike across the Formentor peninsula through the Bóquer valley, a paradise for ornithologists and lovers of wild flowers.

🔁 8B 🍴 Choice of restaurants (€) 🚌 From Palma, Pollença and Alcúdia; also from Port d'Alcúdia and Cap de Formentor in summer ❓ Market held Wed

PORT DE SÓLLER

This small resort, set around a horseshoe-shaped natural harbour, has the only beach of any note along the northwest coast. With an excellent selection of restaurants, stylish bars, a small but informative **museum** and a gorgeous backdrop of wooded hills, it's a delightful place to spend the day. It is also the starting point for several boat trips

along the coast, and is a good base for walks. A climb of less than an hour brings you to Cap Gros lighthouse for panoramic views of the bay and the mountains behind; a longer path connects with an old mule track from Deià to Sóller.

🕀 4C 🍴 Wide choice of restaurants (€–€€€) 🚌 From Palma, Valldemossa and Deià 🚋 From Palma; tram from Sóller

Museu de la Mar

✉ Oratori de Santa Caterina d'Alexandria ☎ 971 630200 🕐 Jun–Sep Tue–Sat 10–2, 5–8; Oct–May Tue–Sat 10–1:30, 3–5 💷 Inexpensive

SA CALOBRA

Do not believe anyone who tells you that they have discovered the perfect unspoiled cove on the north coast – unless it's Sa Calobra. This is such a beautiful spot that tour buses pour in every day.

The journey to Sa Calobra is as memorable as the bay itself. A twisting road around Puig Major plunges 800m (2,625ft) in just 12km (7.5 miles), turning 270 degrees at one point to loop under itself (known as the 'Knotted Tie'). The easier approach is by boat from Port de Sóller (year-round), passing isolated bays with an excellent view of Puig Major.

Once there, walk through 200m (655ft) of tunnels to reach the Torrent de Pareis ('twin streams'), which begins up in the mountains at the confluence of the torrents of Lluc and Gorg Blau. Up to 400m (1,310ft) high and only 30m (100ft) wide in places, with some sections never seeing daylight, this dramatic gorge culminates in a small pebble beach. In summer, when the gorge is dry, you can hike inland between the cliffs.

A side turn off the road to Sa Calobra leads to Cala Tuent, a small cove with a sandy beach and a 13th-century church, Ermita de Sant Llorenç. Cala Tuent is likely to be quieter than Sa Calobra.

🕀 5B 🍴 Restaurants (€–€€) 🚢 From Port de Sóller ☎ 971 630170

SERRA DE TRAMUNTANA

The 'mountains of the north wind' which run the length of Mallorca's northwest coast are home to the island's most spectacular landscapes. Pine-covered slopes almost lean into the sea; as you climb higher, forested hills give way to barren crags and peaks. The people of Mallorca have good reason to be grateful to the mountains. In winter they act as a buffer, shielding the plain from the fierce *tramuntana* wind and absorbing most of the island's rain and snow; in summer they provide a cool retreat from the heat of Palma and the south.

The Serra de Tramuntana for many people is the most enchanting part of the island. It runs for 88km (55 miles) from Andratx (► 106) to Pollença (► 128–129), with the rocky outcrops of Sa Dragonera (► 118) and Cap de Formentor (► 40–41) at either end. It contains Lluc, Mallorca's most sacred site (► 50–51) and Sóller, one of its prettiest towns (► 134–135).

Of the 10 peaks over 1,000m, (3,280ft), most are concentrated in the area around Lluc; the highest are Puig Major (1,445m/4,740ft) and Puig Massanella (1,367m/4,485ft). There are no rivers, though there are several mountain torrents which swell rapidly after rain – and the Cúber and Gorg Blau reservoirs, essential resources on an island so often affected by drought.

The mountains are best seen slowly, on foot. Running the entire length of the mountain chain, the GR221, or Ruta de Pedra en Sec (dry-stone path) is a glorious way to explore this astonishing region of evergreen oaks, pines and juniper bushes. Taking it slowly, you'll be able to hear the sheep bells, smell the wild rosemary and marvel at trees growing out of ochre rock. The route is well waymarked, and a network of eight new *refugis* (hostels) offer comfortable, rustic accommodation along the way.

➕ 1E–7B ℹ️ For information on the GR221, *refugis* and other walking trails, contact the tourist office in Sóller ☎ 971 638008; www.sollernet.com
❓ Walking, birds, spring flowers

SÓLLER

Set in a lush valley of orange groves between the mountains and the sea, Sóller is popular with day trippers who arrive on the vintage train from Palma and seem to do little but sit outside the cafés in Plaça Constitució soaking up the atmosphere and the sun. With several *tapas* bars, a fine selection of pastry shops, local ice cream and freshly squeezed orange juice, there is little reason to move on.

Sóller grew rich on oranges and the results can be seen in its extravagant *modernista* architecture. The church of Sant Bartomeu has a 1912 arched tower suspended above the rose window, with spires like huge needles pointing into the air. The same architect, Gaudí's pupil Joan Rubió, designed the Banco Central Hispano next door.

A stroll to the cemetery above the station, flanked by cypress trees and filled with potted plants, gives a clue to Sóller's history. Several of the epitaphs are in French, revealing the significant

French community of the town, descendants of those who came to make their fortune by exporting oranges.

Sóller has two museums worth visiting. The **Natural Science Museum,** in a turn-of-the-19th-century manor house on the Palma road, has a collection of fossils and a botanical garden. The **Museu de Sóller** is an 18th-century town house in the town centre, filled with antiques and relics of old Sóller.

A final word of advice: come here by train, rather than car. The climb over the

Coll de Sóller, with its 57 hairpin bends, is the most dizzying drive in Mallorca. There is now a controversial new road tunnel through the mountain, but the train journey from Palma is a delight, so why not give yourself a treat.

➕ 4C 🍴 Wide choice of bars and restaurants (€–€€) 🚆 From Palma; tram to Port de Sóller ❓ Market held Sat; *Moros i Cristians*, re-enactment of a 1561 battle in which local women helped to defeat a band of Turkish pirates, 8–10 May

Museu Balear de Ciències Naturals (Natural Science Museum)
✉ Carretera Palma–Port de Sóller ☎ 971 634014; www.jardibotanicdesoller.org 🕐 Tue–Sat 10–6, Sun 10–2 ✋ Inexpensive

Museu de Sóller
✉ Carrer de Sa Mar 9 ☎ 971 634663 🕐 Mon–Fri 11–4, Sat 11–1:30 ✋ Donation

SON MARROIG

Of all the famous foreigners attracted to Mallorca's northwest coast, none is so admired locally as 'S'Arxiduc', Archduke Ludwig Salvator. Born in 1847 in the Pitti Palace, Florence, the son of Leopold III of Tuscany and Marie Antoinette de Bourbon, he came to Mallorca 20 years later to escape from Viennese court life and immediately fell in love with the island. An ecologist before it was fashionable, and an early hippy who wore Mallorcan peasant clothes, he bought up estates along the coast in an effort to save them from development, and devoted himself to studying and recording Mallorcan wildlife and traditions. His seven-volume *Las Baleares* took 20 years to produce and is still an authority on its subject. He died in 1915 in a Bohemian castle.

The Archduke's home at Son Marroig, outside Deià, has been turned into a shrine to his memory, with his photographs, paintings and books and a museum devoted to his life. In the gardens is a white marble rotunda, made from Carrara marble, where you can sit and gaze at the Na Foradada ('pierced rock') peninsula, jutting out to sea with a gaping 18m (59ft) hole at its centre. Ask at the house for permission to stroll down to the peninsula, an hour's walk away.

✚ 3D ✉ Carretera Valldemossa–Deià ☎ 971 639158 🕐 Apr–Sep Mon–Sat 10–7:30; Oct–Mar Mon–Sat 10–5:30 💶 Inexpensive 🍴 Mirador de Na Foradada (€€) 🚌 From Palma, Valldemossa and Port de Sóller

VALLDEMOSSA

Best places to see, ➤ 54–55.

HOTELS

DEIÀ
La Residencia (€€€)
See page 68.

S'Hotel d'Es Puig (€€)
The 'hotel on the hill' featured in a short story by Robert Graves and also in Gordon West's *Jogging Round Majorca*. Small, elegant and central.
✉ Carrer Es Puig 4 ☎ 971 639409; www.hoteldespuig.com 🕐 Closed Jan

Villa Verde (€€)
Close to Deià's hilltop church, this mid-range place has a superb location and sweeping views over the valley towards the Tramuntana hills.
✉ Carrer Ramon Llul 19 ☎ 971 639037; www.hostalvillaverde.com

FORMENTOR
Hotel Formentor (€€€)
A grand hotel in a beautiful setting between the beach and the pine woods, with acres of terraced gardens.
✉ Platja de Formentor ☎ 971 899100; www.hotelformentor.net 🕐 Apr–Oct

FORNALUTX
Ca'n Verdera (€€€)
An old stone house has been tastefully converted into a modern boutique hotel, a great place to relax among the orange groves.
✉ Carrer de Toros 1 ☎ 971 638203; www.canverdera.com

LLUC
Monestir de Lluc (€)
Former monastery that's far from spartan these days, offering surprisingly comfortable (if slightly sparse) rooms and family apartments. The dining room has real baronial charm.
✉ Lluc monastery ☎ 971 871525

ORIENT
L'Hermitage (€€€)
Former convent turned into a magical country-house hotel, with swimming pool, tennis courts, spa facilities and a first-class restaurant.

✉ Carretera Alaró–Bunyola ☎ 971 180303; www.hermitage-hotel.com
🕐 Feb–Nov

POLLENÇA
Juma (€€)
Early 20th-century hotel on the main square with eight comfortable rooms, decorated with antiques and period furnishings.

✉ Plaça Major 9 ☎ 971 535002; www.hoteljuma.com

PORT DE SÓLLER
Es Port (€€)
Family-run *hostal* in a 15th-century mansion.

✉ Carrer Antoni Montis ☎ 971 631650 🕐 Feb–Nov

SÓLLER
Ca'n Roses (€€€)
A sympathetically converted olive mill, this tasteful hotel has a delightfully relaxed air. The individually furnished rooms exude style, and there's a gorgeous garden and rock pool area.

✉ Carrer Quadrado 9 ☎ 971 632299; www.canroses.com 🕐 Jan–Oct

VALLDEMOSSA
Ca'n Mario (€)
Charming family-run *hostal* filled with antiques.

✉ Carrer Uetam 8 ☎ 971 612122

RESTAURANTS

CALA DE SANT VICENÇ
Cavall Bernat (€€€)
Mallorcan dishes, such as spiced turbot and roast sucking lamb.

✉ Carrer Maressers 2 ☎ 971 530250 🕐 Dinner daily

CASTELL D'ALARÓ
Es Verger (€€)
See page 60.

DEIÀ
Bens d'Arvall (€€€)
See page 60.

C'an Quet (€€€)
Just west of the village, this fine restaurant offers cooking with a strong local flavour, using plenty of organic meat sourced in Mallorca.

✉ Carretera Deià–Valldemossa ☎ 971 639196 ◷ Lunch, dinner daily

Jaume (€€)
Offers Mallorcan dishes such as *tumbet* and *frit mallorquí* in defiance of the trend towards new Mediterranean cuisine.

✉ Carrer Arxiduc Lluis Salvador 24 ☎ 971 639029 ◷ Lunch, dinner Tue–Sun

FORNALUTX
Ca'n Antuna (€€)
See page 60.

Es Turó (€€)
A moderately priced menu of good, hearty Mallorcan dishes, and wonderful views from the terrace.

✉ Carrer Arbona Colóm 6 ☎ 971 630808 ◷ Lunch, dinner; closed Thu

JARDINS D'ALFÁBIA
Ses Porxeres (€€)
Catalan game dishes in a barn beside the Alfábia gardens.

✉ Carretera Palma–Sóller ☎ 971 613762 ◷ Lunch, dinner; closed Sun dinner, Mon

ORIENT
Dalt Muntanya (€€)
Pa amb oli at lunchtime and modern Mallorcan cooking in the evening on the terrace of this renovated hotel.

✉ Carretera de Bunyola ☎ 971 615373 ✪ Lunch, dinner daily (Feb–Oct)

Restaurant Orient (€)
Roast lamb, snails and other rustic Mallorcan dishes.

✉ Carretera de Bunyola ☎ 971 615153 ✪ Lunch, dinner; closed Sun dinner, Tue

POLLENÇA
Balaixa (€€)
Dine on the terrace in summer or indoors in winter at this old Mallorcan farmhouse on the main road to Port de Pollença.

✉ Carretera Port de Pollença ☎ 971 530659 ✪ Lunch, dinner daily

Clivia (€€)
This popular restaurant is in an old manor house. Try the local speciality, roasted sea bass.

✉ Avinguda Pollentia 9 ☎ 971 533635 ✪ Lunch, dinner; closed Wed

PORT DE POLLENÇA
Ca'n Cuarassa (€€)
Top-notch Mediterranean cuisine in a delightful setting.

✉ Carretera Port de Pollença-Alcúdia ☎ 971 864266 ✪ Lunch, dinner daily

PORT DE SÓLLER
Celler d'es Port (€€)
Enormous helpings of Mallorcan classics like roast shoulder of lamb with oregano.

✉ Carrer Antoni Montis 17 ☎ 971 630654 ✪ Lunch Thu–Tue, dinner Sat

Es Faro (€€€)
Fresh fish in a magnificent setting, high above the fishing port overlooking the sea. Inexpensive lunch menu.

✉ Cap Gros de Maleta ☎ 971 633752 ✪ Lunch, dinner; closed Tue in winter

Sa Cova (€€)

Tapas and Mallorcan classics (stuffed aubergines and rabbit with garlic) in a great location.

✉ Plaça Constitució 7 ☎ 971 633222 ⊙ Lunch, dinner; closed Sun dinner and Mon

Sa Teulera (€€)

A kilometre or so west of the centre, this buzzing place is packed with locals feasting on *lechona* (sucking pig) and roast lamb.

✉ Carretera Sóller–Pollença, km1 ☎ 971 631111 ⊙ Lunch, dinner Thu–Tue

VALLDEMOSSA
Ca'n Costa (€€)

Mallorcan and Spanish cuisine in a converted oil mill.

✉ Carretera Valldemossa–Deià, km2.5 ☎ 971 612263 ⊙ Lunch, dinner; closed Tue

SHOPPING

Casa Maria

People have been coming for years to Casa Maria for the beautiful hand embroideries on sale here. Bold designs on white linen decorate tablecloths and napkins in striking primary colours.

✉ Passeig Saralegui 86, Port de Pollença

Eugenio

Gifts carved from olive wood – salad bowls, salt cellars, chess sets.

✉ Carrer Jerónimo Estades 11A, Sóller ☎ 971 630984

Lina

This is a great place to look for leather goods including bags, belts and shoes.

✉ Economo Torres 5, Port de Pollença

Sa Posada d'Artesa

Sells some terrific handmade ceramics and glassware.

✉ Carrer Marina 46, Port de Sóller ☎ 971 631313

WEEKLY MARKETS

Calvià – Mon
Pollença – Sun
Port de Pollença – Wed
Sóller – Sat
Valldemossa – Sun

ENTERTAINMENT

DINNER SHOW
Son Amar

Equestrian shows, big bands, flamenco and magic tricks at one of Mallorca's top cabaret shows, in a 16th-century mansion.

✉ Carretera Palma–Sóller, km11, near Bunyola ☎ 971 753614; www.sonamar.com ⏰ Apr–Oct, dinner from 8, show 9

THEATRE AND CONCERTS
Costa Nord

Top names in flamenco, salsa and jazz perform here during the Mediterranean Nights Festival (summer). Also hosts some winter concerts (▶ 125–126).

✉ Avinguda Palma 6, Valdemossa ☎ 971 612425; www.costanord.com

Reial Cartoixa

Chopin festival held each August in the Royal Carthusian Monastery (▶ 55).

✉ Valldemossa ☎ 971 612106; www.festivalchopin.com

Sant Domingo Convent

The cloisters of this 17th-century monastery make a delightful setting for Pollença's international music festival (summer).

✉ Carrer Sant Domingo, Pollença ☎ 971 534012

Son Marroig

Concerts on summer evenings in the gardens. Venue for Deià's classical music festival (▶ 136).

✉ Carretera Valldemossa–Deià ☎ 971 639158; www.sonmarroig.com

The Northeast

Alcúdia

Mallorca's northeastern corner has a beautiful coastline, with arguably the island's best beaches, as well as the historic and characterful towns of Alcúdia and Artà. The area is quieter than other parts of the island and attracts families to its long sandy beaches rather than the clubbers and hedonists that flock to Palma Bay. The dunes and marshlands, including the S'Albufera wetlands (▶ 152–153) attract birdwatchers from all over Europe and the cave system at Artà is another draw to the region.

However, Artà and Alcùdia all come to life on market day when the streets are filled with people and stalls selling food, fruit, souvenirs and pottery, as well as many other goods.

ALCÚDIA

Best places to see, ➤ 36–37.

ARTÀ

Derived from the Arabic word *jertan* ('garden'), Artà has been occupied for at least 3,000 years, as evidenced by the remains of a Bronze Age site at Ses Païsses (➤ 153) just outside the town. Nowadays Artà is a prosperous, attractive and easy-going little place, which gets particularly lively each Tuesday on market day.

From the parish church of Transfiguració del Senyor, an avenue of cypress trees leads to Artà's crowning glory, its hilltop fortress and Santuari de Sant Salvador. The view down over the rooftops, a jumble of tiles in every shade of brown, is one of the sights of Mallorca. On the site of a Moorish fortress, the original sanctuary

walls and chapel were rebuilt in the 19th century. Walk around the battlements, rest in a peaceful courtyard, then look into the sanctuary church with its vivid paintings of two Mallorcan heroes – Jaume the Conqueror receiving the surrender of the *walis*, and Ramón Llull being stoned to death in Tunisia. There is also a painting of Sant Antoni, patron saint of Artà, and of animals, seen here, as always, with a small pig. Each January the saint is commemorated with a masked procession and a blessing of pets. Artà's big festival, Sant Antoni de Juny, dates back to 1581 and features dancers with cardboard horses strapped to their hips.

The coastline north of Artà contains some of Mallorca's wildest and most beautiful beaches, including the virgin cove of Cala Torta.

✚ 11D ⑪ Several bars and restaurants (€–€€) 🚌 From Palma and Cala Rajada ❓ Market held Tue; Sant Antoni Abat, procession and blessing of pets, 16–17 Jan; Sant Antoni de Juny, *cavallets* horse dances, 13 Jun

CALA MILLOR

Just over 50 years ago this was a lonely dune-covered shore; now it has become the major attraction on Mallorca's east coast. The main attraction is its fine sandy beaches; from Cala Bona ('the good bay') to Cala Millor ('the better bay') they stretch unbroken for 2km (1.2 miles). In summer it is 'lively', travel-agent speak for brash, and best avoided unless you're into clubbing and late-night bars; in winter it takes on a new atmosphere, as a resort for the 'young at heart', another travel-agent euphemism. To see what this coast used to be like, walk to the headland at Punta de n'Amer (➤ 151).

✚ 11E ⁋ Wide choice of bars and restaurants (€–€€) 🚌 From Palma; also from Cala Rajada and Port d'Alcúdia in summer

CALA RAJADA

This fishing port on Mallorca's eastern tip, surrounded by fine beaches and pretty coves, is a popular summer resort, with windsurfing, snorkelling and numerous discos. Many Germans have second homes here.

A walk of about 2km (1.2 miles) from the harbour leads through pine woods and crosses a headland to the lighthouse at Punta de Capdepera, the easternmost point on Mallorca. There are also several good beaches within easy reach. The town beach, Son Moll, is often crowded, but for more isolation you can head north to the small cove of Cala Gat or the broad sweep of Cala Agulla.

The other reason for coming here is to make a day trip to Menorca (➤ 28). Boats leave each morning for the Menorcan city of Ciutadella, with its cathedral and harbourside fish restaurants.

✚ 12D ⁋ Wide choice of restaurants (€€) 🚌 From Palma and Porto Cristo; also from Cala Millor in summer 🚢 Day trips to Menorca ☎ 902 100444

❓ Market held Sat; processions of boats, 16 July

ℹ Plaça dels Pins ☎ 971 563033

CAPDEPERA

If you are driving between Artà and Cala Rajada, stop off to visit this small town, crowned by the largest fortress in Mallorca. The Romans were the first to build a **castle** on this site – the Moors enlarged it, the Christians destroyed it, then replaced it with one of their own in the 14th century. Legend has it that the citizens of Capdepera hid in the castle when under siege, placing an image of Our Lady of Hope on the battlements, and the invaders were driven away by fog. The miracle is recorded inside the castle in the Capella de Nostra Senyora de la Esperança and remembered each year at the town's annual *festa*. You reach the castle by climbing the steps from the market square, Plaça de l'Orient.

🕂 11D 🍴 Café de l'Orient, Plaça de l'Orient (€) 🚌 From Palma and Cala Rajada 🚻 Market held Wed; Nostra Senyora de la Esperança *festa*, 18 Dec

Castle

☎ 971 818746 🕓 Apr–Oct daily 10–8; Nov–Mar daily 10–5 🖐 Inexpensive

COVES D'ARTÀ

Best places to see, ➤ 44–45.

MURO

This small town between Inca and the S'Albufera marshes has one overriding attraction – the **Museu Etnòlogic de Mallorca.** Housed in a former mansion, it gives fascinating glimpses into Mallorca's past. Upstairs there is a fine collection of *siurells* (clay whistles) featuring men on horseback, carrying water and playing guitars and some old Mallorcan bagpipes. A courtyard with a well, a waterwheel and orange trees leads to more exhibits – blacksmith's and cobbler's workshops, a collection of carriages, and tools once used by silversmiths, sculptors and spoonmakers.

The Catalan-Gothic church of Sant Joan Baptista looks almost Arabic, guarded by palm trees and a tall, square bell-tower linked to the main church by a tiny bridge. Rebuilt in the 16th century, it has a colourful rose window over the west door. Another church, the convent of Santa Anna, used to stage fights between bulls and bulldogs, and bullfights can still be seen at the Plaça de Toros, built out of white stone in its own quarry in 1910.

Sa Pobla, 4km (2.5 miles) north of Muro, is Mallorca's vegetable basket; this fertile area of marshes reclaimed as farmland is referred to as 'the land of a thousand windmills'. It is also the home of one of Mallorca's most unusual festivals, the Revelta de Sant Antoni. For two days each January pets are led through the town to be blessed outside the church, dancers drive out the Devil for the coming year, and everyone eats pastries filled with spicy spinach and marsh eels.

✚ 8D ❓ Sun market; Revelta de Sant Antoni, 16–17 Jan 🚉 Train from Palma

Museu Etnòlogic de Mallorca

✉ Carrer Major 15 ☎ 971 717540 🕐 Tue–Sat 10–3, Sun 10–2
🖐 Inexpensive

PORT D'ALCÚDIA

As the name suggests, this was once a port serving
a city; now the port has completely outgrown the
town. The biggest of the resorts on Mallorca's
northeast coast, it stands at the head of a 10km
(6-mile) stretch of sandy beach which continues
around the bay of Alcúdia as far as Can Picafort. The
whole strip has been developed for tourism but the
area around the fishing harbour is the most
attractive, with some fine seafood restaurants. Near
here is the commercial port, where passenger
ferries leave for the Menorcan city of Ciutadella.

➕ 8B 🍴 Wide choice of restaurants (€€) 🚌 From Palma
and Alcúdia; also from Port de Pollença in summer

PUIG DE MARIA

Climb for an hour out of Pollença, or drive up a
terrifying potholed road, and you are rewarded with
views over Cap de Formentor and the entire
northeastern coast – as well as back down over Pollença. Nuns
settled on Puig de Maria ('Mary's mountain') in 1371 and remained
for several hundred years, refusing to leave even when the Bishop
of Palma ordered them down for their own safety. The convent is
still there, on top of the mountain; the chapel smells of incense

and the refectory
of woodsmoke.
You can stay in
simple cells in the
sanctuary here,
but don't expect
luxury – unless you
count waking to a
view of sunrise
over Pollença Bay.

The caretaker will rustle up a meal to save you the long walk back to town.

✚ 7B ☎ 971 184132 🍴 Bar-restaurant (€) 🚌 From Palma to Pollença
✋ Free

PUNTA DE N'AMER

This 200ha (495-acre) nature reserve on a headland jutting out from the east coast is an oasis of peace amid an onslaught of high-rise apartments and hotels. Once, the whole coast was like this – thankfully, environmentalists have saved this small section from development. Walk south from Cala Millor, or north from Sa Coma, on a well-defined 1.5km (1-mile) track. Eventually you reach the Castell de n'Amer, a 17th-century watchtower. Have a drink at the summit and look down at what you have left behind.

✚ 24H 🍴 Snack bar (€) 🚌 From Palma to Cala Millor ✋ Free

S'ALBUFERA

Just off the coast road 5km (3 miles) south of Port d'Alcúdia, the Parc Natural de S'Albufera wetlands make a welcome relief from crowded beaches. Birdwatchers come to see rare migrants like Montagu's harriers and Eleonora's falcons; herons and cranes are common, while species breeding here include stonechats, moustached warblers and long-eared owls. Ospreys leave their breeding sites on the cliffs to come here to fish; peregrines and hoopoes live here all year round.

The name derives from the Arabic for 'lagoon', but the site has been exploited since Roman times – Pliny writes of night herons, probably from S'Albufera, being sent to Rome as a gastronomic delicacy. The wetlands were drained for agriculture in the 19th century by a British company which subsequently went bankrupt; the network of canals dates from this time. Rice was introduced in the early 20th century, paper was manufactured from the reeds and sedge, and it is only since 1985, following fears that tourist development was damaging the area's fragile ecology, that S'Albufera has been a protected nature reserve. There are

footpaths, cycle trails, bird-watching hides and audiovisual display room where you can listen to birdsong.

➕ 8C ✉ Carretera Port d'Alcúdia–Artà, km5 ☎ 971 892250 🕐 Apr–Sep daily 9–6; Oct–Mar daily 9–5 🍴 Picnic area 🚌 From Port d'Alcúdia to Cala Rajada in summer 🎫 Free ❓ Cars not allowed in the reserve – leave them 1km (0.5 miles) from the visitor centre on the main road in the car park opposite Hotel Parc Natural

SES PAÏSSES

Although not as extensive as the ruins at Capocorb Vell (➤ 162–163), this Bronze Age settlement near Artà is still a significant site and a link with Mallorcans of 3,000 years ago. Most impressive of all is the massive entrance portal, formed from three stone slabs weighing up to eight tonnes each. Inside there are several rooms and an *atalaia* (watchtower); the entire settlement is surrounded by a Cyclopean drystone wall.

➕ 11D 🕐 Apr–Oct Mon–Sat 9:30–1, 4–7:30; Nov–Mar Mon–Fri 9–1, 2–5 🎫 Inexpensive 🚌 From Cala Rajada or Palma then short walk

HOTELS

ALCÚDIA
Es Convent (€€€)

One of the most memorable hotels in the north of Mallorca. Four tastefully decorated rooms and a superb restaurant in a pair of stone houses in the heart of Alcúdia's old town.

✉ Carrer Progrès 6 ☎ 971 548716; www.esconvent.com ⏰ Feb–Nov

Son Siurana (€€€)

One of Mallorca's finest *agroturismos*, once a grand *finca*, nestling in foothills just outside Alcúdia. The apartments and *casitas* have real rustic character, and the pool and sun terraces are wonderful.

✉ Carretera Palma–Alcúdia km45 ☎ 971 549662; www.sonsiurana.com ⏰ Mar–Dec

ARTÀ
Ca'n Moragues (€€)

Just eight rooms and a heated swimming pool and sauna in this stylish, renovated, 18th-century town house. There's an attractive courtyard with orange trees, ideal for breakfast. Several golf courses are within a short drive of Artà

✉ Carrer Pou Nou 12 ☎ 971 829509; www.canmoragues.com

CALA RAJADA
Ses Rotges (€€)

Historic villa in a quiet area of town, with a beautiful flower-filled garden and a Michelin-starred restaurant (➤ opposite).

✉ Carrer Rafael Blanes 21 ☎ 971 563108; www.sesrotges.com ⏰ Apr–Oct

RESTAURANTS

ALCÚDIA
Ca'n Simó (€€)

Stylish vegetarian cooking in a chic town-house hotel. The four-course lunch menu is excellent value, while dinner is a slightly more elaborate affair.

✉ Carrer d'en Serra 22 ☎ 971 542673; www.cansimo.com ⏰ Lunch, dinner; closed Mon

Es Convent (€€€)

The restaurant at the Es Convent hotel (➤ opposite) attracts diners in its own right. The menu changes seasonally and there is an extensive wine list.

✉ Carrer Progrès 6 ☎ 971 548716 🕔 Lunch, dinner; closed Mon

Sa Plaça (€€)

Traditional and modern Spanish and Mediterranean cuisine in an elegant restaurant on the main square in Alcúdia. Try the courgettes stuffed with pine nuts, raisins, black pudding and Mallorcan cheese.

✉ Plaça Constitució 1 ☎ 971 546278 🕔 Thu–Tue 12–12

ARTÀ
Café Parisien (€€)

This is the most attractive and welcoming of Artà's café-bar-restaurants on the main street, serving tapas, pastries, salads and Mediterranean cuisine. Upstairs you'll find deli food and wine from Mallorca.

✉ Carrer Ciutat 18 ☎ 971 835440 🕔 Lunch, dinner daily

CALA RAJADA
Ses Rotges (€€€)

One of the most successful restaurants on the island. Quality French cooking using fresh, local ingredients with prices to match at one of Mallorca's top hotels (➤ opposite).

✉ Carrer Rafael Blanes 21 ☎ 971 563108 🕔 Lunch, dinner daily; closed Nov–Mar

CAPDEPERA
Café de l'Orient (€)

Lively *tapas* bar on the market square.

✉ Plaça de l'Orient 4 ☎ 971 563098 🕔 Daily 8am–midnight

PORT D'ALCÚDIA
Bogavante (€€€)
The rice and fresh fish dishes are especially good at this seafood restaurant facing the harbour. The *paella* is superb here.

✉ Carrer Teodor Canet 2 ☎ 971 547364 🕐 Lunch, dinner; closed Mon

Mirador de la Victòria (€€€)
It's worth the drive out for the stunning views from the terrace of this restaurant, beside the 17th-century Santuari de la Victòria. The chicken dishes and grilled rabbit are recommended.

✉ Adjacent to Santuari de la Victòria, Cap des Pinar ☎ 971 547173
🕐 Lunch, dinner; closed Mon, Dec and Jan

ENTERTAINMENT

DISCO
Menta
Designed like a Roman temple around an open-air pool, it honours Alcúdia's history each May with a 'Roman orgy'.

✉ Avinguda Argentina, Port d'Alcúdia ☎ 971 891972; www.mentadisco.com
🕐 11pm–6am; nightly in summer, weekends in winter

THEATRES AND CONCERTS
Auditori d'Alcúdia
A stunning hall, hosting concerts and drama, surrounded by the city's finest hotels, restaurants and bars.

✉ Plaça de la Porta de Mallorca 3, Alcúdia ☎ 971 897185

Sa Màniga
One of Mallorca's principal auditoriums featuring a programme of regular concerts, exhibitions, operas, shows and theatre productions.

✉ Carrer Son Galta 4, Cala Millor ☎ 971 587373

Inland, East and the South

The rural heartland of Mallorca lies to the south and is seemingly untouched by the tourist invasions of the coastal towns further north. Agricultural activity dominates the area and there is no more impressive a sight than the blanket of pretty white almond blossom that carpets the countryside in February each year. The flat plain, Es Pla, is a patchwork of orchards and almond groves with some hills dotted here and there where you will find villages and towns of the 'real Mallorca'. This area attracts a lot of investment from foreign buyers, and some country hotels are springing up, but for the most part it remains unspoiled and a peaceful place to wander along the country lanes that were laid down in Roman times.

☐ Llucmajor

Cabrera

On the southeast coast there are some busy resorts such as Cala d'Or, with Porto Cristo on the east coast, but the coastline is quite rugged and some of the beaches and coves are only accessible by boat. Further offshore the island of Cabrera is home to a wide range of seabirds and wildlife including Mediterranean turtles.

Inset map: *Illa de Cabrera*

ALGAIDA

Algaida is a typical Mallorcan town, all green shutters, narrow streets, a square lined with cafés and a huge sandstone church. Few visitors make it into the town centre; the attractions are all on the outskirts, on the Palma–Manacor road. The main one is **Ca'n Gordiola** (➤ 78), a glass factory in a mock castle. The ground floor contains a workshop (though it looks more like a church with its arches and stained glass) where you can watch glass being blown; upstairs there is a museum devoted to the history of glass-making. A further 2km (1.2 miles) along the road to Manacor is a string of well-known restaurants, where the people of Palma head at weekends for traditional Mallorcan cuisine.

➕ 19H ▮ Restaurants on the Palma–Manacor road (€) 🚌 From Palma
❓ Market held Fri

Ca'n Gordiola

✉ Carretera Palma–Manacor, km19 ☎ 971 665046 🕓 Apr–Oct Mon–Sat 9–6, Sun 9–12; Nov–Mar Mon–Sat 9–1:30, 3–6, Sun 9–12 ✋ Free

BINISSALEM

If you order Mallorcan wine in a restaurant, it will probably come from Binissalem. Viticulture was introduced by the Romans and has survived in much reduced form. The reputation of Binissalem red wines, made with the local grape Manto Negro, has been growing recently – you can visit the best-known *bodega*, **José L Ferrer.** Binissalem has a handsome historic centre, particularly in the streets around the church square.

➕ 5D 🍴 Several restaurants and bars (€€) 🚆 Train from Palma and Inca
❓ Market held Fri; wine festival last weekend in Sep

José L Ferrer

✉ Carrer Conquistador 103 ☎ 971 511050; www.vinosferrer.com
🕐 Mon–Fri 9–7, Sat 10–2 ✋ Guided tours moderate; also offers tastings

CABRERA, ILLA DE

'Goat Island' is the largest in a rocky archipelago 10km (6 miles) off the south coast. During the Napoleonic Wars it was a notorious prison camp. Since 1991 the island has been a protected national park. You can only get there on a day trip, with time to walk up to the 14th-century castle, visit a museum housed in an old wine cellar and swim in the Blue Grotto on the way back.

➕ 14L 🚢 From Colònia de Sant Jordi, Apr–Oct daily 9:30 (☎ 971 649034

CALA D'OR

Each of the various *calas* (bays) along the east coast has its own distinctive character; in the case of Cala d'Or the word is 'chic'. Former fishing harbours have been turned into marinas; people come here to sail and dive, and drink champagne at waterfront bars. The villas are white and flat-roofed, designed in the 1930s by Pep Costa Ferrer, and the effect is surprisingly attractive.

Nowadays Cala d'Or is the collective name for a string of resorts, beaches and coves; they include Porto Petro, around a horseshoe bay 2km (1.2 miles) to the south, and idyllic Cala Santanyí 8km (5 miles) farther on. Perhaps the least developed and most peaceful cove here is Cala Mondragó, where a pair of sandy beaches form part of the Mondragó nature reserve.

➕ 22K 🍽 Wide choice of restaurants (€€–€€€) 🚌 From Palma

CALA FIGUERA

More than anywhere else in Mallorca, Cala Figuera retains the atmosphere of a working fishing port. White-painted houses reach down to the water's edge and fishermen sit on the steps mending nets. If you get here early enough in the morning you might even see the catch coming in. A path follows around the tiny harbour and onto the cliffs, offering good views back towards the bay. The nearest beach is 4km (2.5 miles) to the south at Cala Santanyí.

🕂 22L 🍽 Several seafood restaurants and others (€€) 🚌 From Palma and Santanyí

CAMPOS

Midway from Llucmajor to Santanyí on the C717, Campos was founded by Jaume II in 1300 on the site of earlier Roman and Arab settlements. A painting of Christ by the Sevillian artist Murillo hangs in the **parish church of Sant Julià.** Next door to the church is a museum with a large collection of offertory bowls. To visit both the church and the museum, meet the parish priest

outside the church door at 11am for a guided tour. Campos has a busy market on Thursdays and Saturdays and its port adjoins the resort of Colònia de Sant Jordi (▶ 163) to the south.

🕂 20K 🍽 Several cafés and bars (€) 🚌 From Palma

Església de Sant Julià

✉ Carrer Bisbe Talladas 17 ☎ 971 650003 🕐 Mon–Sat 11am 🖐 Donation

CAPOCORB VELL

These are the most significant remains of the Talaiotic culture, which flourished in Mallorca between around 1300 and 800BC. Villages were dominated by *talaiots*, circular or rectangular structures two to three storeys high, which were used as both burial chambers and defensive forts. Each settlement was surrounded by Cyclopean walls, built from massive, unhewn stones without mortar to hold them together. There is no evidence of a written language, so the stones are all that archaeologists have to go on in understanding prehistoric Mallorcan culture. At Capocorb Vell, 12km (7.5 miles) south of Llucmajor, you can see five *talaiots* and wander around the ancient village, 100m (330ft) above sea level just inland from the coast. The Talaiotic people kept sheep, and the sound of sheep bells in the nearby fields is a touching reminder of continuity.

✚ 18K 🖂 Carretera Cap Blanc–Llucmajor
☎ 971 180155 🕐 Fri–Wed 10–5 ✋ Inexpensive
🍴 Nearby (€)

COLÒNIA DE SANT JORDI

Once the port for the market town of Campos, Colònia de Sant Jordi is now a busy resort, on a rocky promontory close to Mallorca's southern tip. Its small beach looks out over several islets, with good views all the way to Cabrera (➤ 159). There are two further sandy beaches to the east, and the long stretch of Platja Es Trenc begins just west of town. To the north are the hot springs of Banys de Sant Joan. The main reason for coming here, though, is to take the boat trip to Cabrera.

✚ 20L 🍴 Choice of restaurants (€–€€€)
🚌 From Palma ❓ Market held Wed

COVES DEL DRAC

Dank, dark and humid, the limestone Dragon Caves on the edge of Porto Cristo have become one of Mallorca's top tourist sights. Groups of several hundred people at a time are herded along 2km (1.2 miles) of slippery paths by guides who tell you in four languages how to interpret the bizarre stalactite formations – a cactus here, a flag there, the Fairies' Theatre, Diana's Bath... You might just think they resemble thousands of spiky parsnips hanging from the ceiling. Try to imagine how Walt Disney would conjure up a fabulous witches' cave and you have the idea. The one-hour tour ends with a floodlit, floating violin concert on Lake Martel, at 175m (575ft) long Europe's largest underground lake. There's also a small aquarium with tanks of Mediterranean sealife and a few exotic fishes. Afterwards you can return by boat across the lake to the exit.

✚ 23H ☎ 971 820753; www.cuevasdrach.com ⏰ Apr–Oct, tours on the hour 10–5; Nov–Mar, tours at 10:45, 12, 2, 3:30 ✋ Expensive 🍴 Café (€)
🚌 From Palma and Cala Rajada

COVES DELS HAMS

You cannot miss these caves as you drive from Manacor to Porto Cristo. Most people only want to visit one set of caves and the giant billboards and flags at the entrance are an attempt to ensure that this is the one. In fact you are better off continuing to the Coves del Drac (➤ above) or up the coast to the Coves d'Artà (➤ 44–45).

But for serious speleologists, here are the facts. The caves were discovered by Pedro Caldentey in 1905 and the electric lighting was added by his son. Their name means 'fish-hooks', which the stalactites are said to resemble. You get a guided tour and, yes, another concert on an underground lake.

✚ 23H ✉ Carretera Manacor–Porto Cristo ☎ 971 820988; www.cuevas-hams.com ⏰ Apr–Oct daily 10–6; Nov–Mar daily 10:30–5 ✋ Expensive
🍴 Café-restaurant (€)

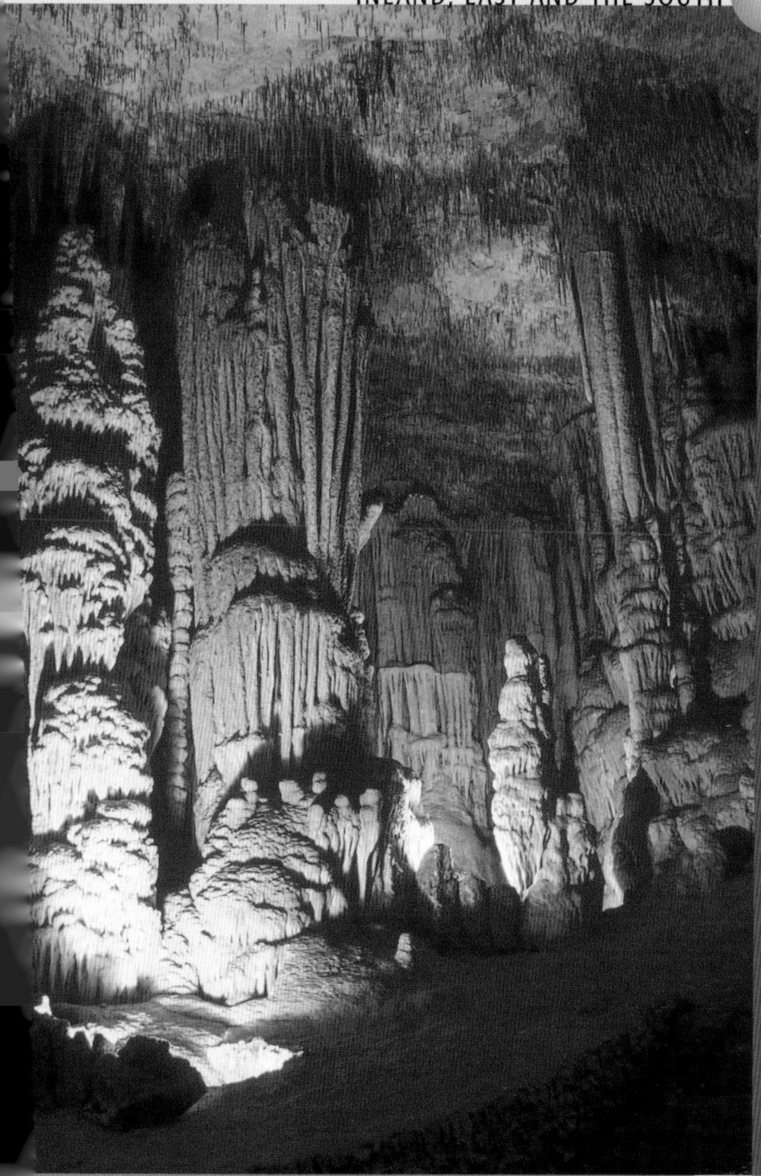

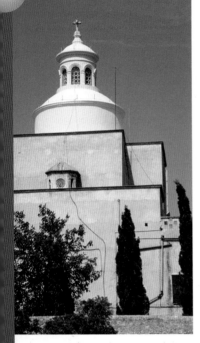

ERMITA DE BONANY

This hilltop hermitage is where Junípero Serra preached his last sermon in Mallorca before leaving to found the Mexican and Californian missions. The views from the terrace, covering almost the entire plain, are superb. You can stay here in simple cells, but unlike other monasteries it has no restaurant or bar – just a chapel and a small shop selling religious trinkets.

✚ 21H ☎ 971 561101
✋ Free

FELANITX

Felanitx is at the centre of Mallorca's second wine-producing area and it is also known for its capers, or 'green pearls'. You can buy them at the Sunday morning market, in the streets around the church of Sant Miquel, with local pottery displayed on the church steps. The church facade contains a memorial to 414 people who died when a wall collapsed in 1844; further up, beneath the rose window, is the archangel Michael standing on the Devil's head.

➕ 22J 🍴 Bars and cafés (€) 🚌 From Palma and Porto Colom ❓ Market held Sun; Sant Agusti, *cavallets* horse dances, 28 Aug

INCA

Mallorca's third-largest town is an industrial place that styles itself as a 'city of leather', and if you come on an organized tour you will undoubtedly be taken to a leather factory. Shop around; the bargains these days are few and far between. Come on Thursdays, when the streets around Plaça d'Espanya are taken over by Mallorca's largest weekly market. There's plenty of leather here, of varying quality, plus jewellery, carved olive-wood, lace and fresh produce from across the island.

Plaça d'Espanya itself becomes an open-air flower show. Near here are a smart coffee-house, Café Mercantil, with upholstered leather chairs, and Ca'n Delante (tel: Carrer Major 27), one of Mallorca's top pastry shops. Inca is also known for its *cellers*, old wine-cellars turned into restaurants featuring traditional dishes at reasonable prices.

➕ 6D 🍴 Wide choice of restaurants (€) 🚌 From Palma 🚆 From Palma

LLUCMAJOR

This ordinary country town, the largest in southern Mallorca, has a place in history – it was the site of the battle in 1349 where Pedro IV of Aragón killed his relative Jaume III to end Mallorca's brief spell as an independent kingdom. Jaume's death is commemorated by a statue at the end of Passeig Jaume III. Nearby, on Carrer Obispo Taxaquet, is another statue in honour of Llucmajor's cobblers. Shoemaking is still a significant industry here, and the town has few sights. Almonds and apricots grow around the town and make good buys at the market, held twice a week in Plaça d'Espanya.

🔢 19J 🍴 Cafés and bars (€) 🚌 From Palma
❓ Market held Wed, Sun

MANACOR

Mallorca's second city is an industrial town that's most famous for being the home of tennis superstar Rafael Nadal. The narrow streets behind the church make a pleasant place to stroll and soak up the atmosphere of everyday Mallorca. The church, Església dels Delors de Nostra Senyora, was built on the site of a mosque and its minaret-style tower can be seen from afar. Look inside to see the figure of Christ with scrawny hair and a skirt – pilgrims queue up to kiss his bloodstained feet.

Almost every visitor to Manacor ends up at a pearl factory – **Perlas Majórica** is the best-known. Mallorca's artificial pearl industry produces 50 million pearls a year, using the scales of a million fish, so do not imagine they are a safe alternative for your vegetarian friends.

✚ 22H 🍴 Several bars and cafés (€) 🚌 From Palma and Porto Cristo ❓ Market held Mon

Perlas Majórica

✉ Avinguda Majórica 48 ☎ 971 550200 🕐 Mon–Fri 9–7, Sat–Sun 10–1 ✋ Free

MONTUÏRI

High on a ridge surrounded by old stone windmills, the village of Montuïri is probably the most impressive sight along the Palma–Manacor road. The eight mill-towers of the Molinar district, redundant since the 1920s, are the symbol of the village; the best views are from the Ermita de Sant Miquel, a 19th-century hermitage on top of a small hill 2km (1.2 miles) to the east. Montuïri is the setting for one of Mallorca's most spectacular festivals: each August *Cossiers*, accompanied by dancers with bagpipes, flutes and drums, dress up as women and devils and perform a dance, the origins of which stretch back at least 400 years, where evil is overcome by good.

✚ 20H 🍴 Restaurants and bars (€) 🚌 From Palma ❓ Market on Mon; Sant Bartomeu festival, 24 Aug; Fira de la Perdiu (partridge and hunting fair), first Sun in Dec

PETRA

This sleepy town of sand-coloured houses would be completely off the tourist map if it were not the birthplace of Mallorca's most famous son, Fray Junípero Serra. Born in 1713, he became a priest in 1730 and worked as a missionary in Mexico from 1749 to 1763. At the age of 54 he was sent to California; the missions he established there grew into some of the USA's largest cities, including San Diego and San Francisco.

You can visit the **house** where Serra's parents lived, a **museum** devoted to his life and work and the nearby San Bernardino convent where he went to school. A plaque outside the parish church describing him as 'explorer, missionary, hero, civiliser'. Anyone walking down the street leading to his birthplace, decorated with majolica tiles depicting him baptizing Native Americans, might be inclined to disagree, but by the standards of his day he was certainly a hero.

✚ 8E 🍴 Es Celler restaurant (€€); bars on main square (€) 🚉 Train from Palma ❓ Market held Wed

Serra House and Museum

✉ Carrer Barracar Alt ☎ 971 561149 🕐 By arrangement – follow the directions to the keyholder's house 💰 Donation requested

PLATJA DE PALMA

This 5km (3-mile) stretch of fine white sand is just minutes from the airport. The two resorts of Can Pastilla and S'Arenal have merged into one, connected by a palm-lined promenade. It's a good resort for families – there are children's playgrounds and a miniature train ride, though the nightlife can get a bit raucous. Take a *passeig* (promenade) here before dinner and you will have a fabulous view of the twinkling lights of Palma.

🚌 17J 🍴 Bars and restaurants (€–€€) 🚍 Regular buses from Palma

PORRERES

Porreres is typical of the small towns on the Mallorcan plain – nothing much to see, but an easy-going atmosphere and a good place to while away a couple of hours. The main street, Avinguda Bisbe Campins, runs from the church to the town hall and is lined with bars and cafés. A former hospital contains the **Museu i Fons Artistic,** with works by Salvador Dalí. Outside town is a former hilltop hermitage, Santuari de Montesió, with a simple chapel, irregular cloisters and views across the plain and out to sea.

🚌 20J 🍴 Choice of restaurants and bars (€) ❓ Market held Tue

Museu i Fons Artistic

✉ Carrer Reverend Agustí Font 23 ☎ 971 647221 🕐 Tue, Sat 11–2; also temporary exhibitions Fri–Sun 7pm–9pm ✋ Free

a drive

around the Central Plain

This lovely drive criss-crosses the central plain (Es Pla), following old Roman roads through almond and apricot groves and vineyards on its way to a number of small market towns.

Start in Petra by the parish church, following signs to Felanitx. On the way out of the village, you pass the road leading up to Ermita de Bonany (▶ 166), where the views are splendid across the plain.

Keep straight ahead at a roundabout to cross over the C715, the main road from Palma to Manacor. Stay on this country road for 7km (4 miles), then turn left towards Felanitx (▶ 166–167). When you see the town ahead of you, take a sharp right turn, signposted to Porreres.

Follow this road across fertile countryside for 12km (7.5 miles) and into the centre of Porreres (▶ 171), which is

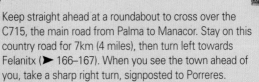

a good place to stop for lunch with its numerous bars and cafés.

Leaving Porreres, follow signs to Llucmajor. Stay on this road for 12km (7.5 miles) as farmland gradually gives way to woods. Reaching Llucmajor (► 168) – with its Wednesday and Saturday market – turn left at the roundabout and stay on the ring road to the far end of town; turn right, following signs to Algaida.

The road rises and falls for 8km (5 miles) around the foot of Puig de Randa (► 176–177), a highlight of Mallorca with its sense of history and religious connotations. When you reach Algaida (► 158), turn right to briefly join the C715 to Manacor. After 1km (0.5 miles), turn left towards Pina and stay on this rural road through Pina and Lloret de Vista Alegre, with views of the sierra in the distance as you head for Sineu (► 181). Here you can visit the modern art gallery, S'Estació, in an old station.

Just before entering Sineu (come on a Wednesday morning for one of Mallorca's most traditional markets), turn right to skirt the town centre and turn right again to return to Petra on the old road.

Distance 80km (50 miles)
Time 2 hours
Start/end point Petra ✚ 8E
Lunch Centro (€) ✉ Avinguda Bisbe Campins, Porreres
☎ 971 168372

173

PORTO COLOM

This fishing village, once the port for Felanitx, was named in honour of Christopher Columbus, who is said – without much evidence – to have been born here. Until the late 19th century Porto Colom was busy supplying wine to France; but when phylloxera killed the vines, its role as a port diminished though it has now discovered a life as a tourist resort. Popular with Mallorcan and Spanish visitors and set inside a deep natural harbour, it still has the feel of a small fishing port, with boats around the quay and pastel-coloured houses lining the waterfront, each with its own landing stage. Cala Marçal, 2km (1.2 miles) south, has a wide sandy beach leading to a narrow rocky cove.

23K   Choice of restaurants (€€)   From Palma and Felanitx

PORTO CRISTO

This was one of the main resorts on the east coast until Cala Millor came along. So much the better: with bigger and better beaches elsewhere, Porto Cristo has carved out a role as a friendly, family resort, taking advantage of a superb position at the end of a long, sheltered inlet. Once the port for Manacor, Porto Cristo was the only place in Mallorca to be caught up in the Spanish Civil War, when it was briefly captured by Republican forces in 1936. There is not much to do but swim, sunbathe and dine at the terrace restaurants, which are perfectly placed to catch the lunchtime sun – but day trippers come in droves to visit the nearby Coves del Drac (➤ 164).

➕ 24H 🍴 Wide choice of restaurants (€€) 🚌 From Palma and Manacor ❓ Market held Sun

PÒRTOL

The neighbouring villages of Pòrtol and Sa Cabaneta, between Palma and Santa María del Camí, have become something of an artists' colony. Unlike in Deià and Banyalbufar, though, the artists are Mallorcan – potters taking advantage of the rich local soil. The only real reason for coming here is to visit the ollerías (workshops), where prices are much lower than in the tourist shops. Good buys include greixoneras (heavy earthenware cooking pots) and ollas (clay storage jars), as well as simple but attractive brown-glazed plates and plats morenos, glazed bowls painted with symbols (some of the designs go back to Arab times). Several artists specialize in the miniature earthenware figures known as siurells, which incorporate a crude whistle in the base.

➕ 5E 🍴 Bars (€) 🚌 From Palma ❓ Market held Thu; Fira del Fang, annual pottery fair held in Mar in the nearby town of Marratxí

PUIG DE RANDA

This table mountain, rising 540m (1,771ft) out of the plain, has been a place of pilgrimage ever since Ramón Llull founded Mallorca's first hermitage here in 1275. He came aged 40, shaken by an incident which caused him to review his way of life. Bent on seduction he chased a married woman through Palma on horseback; unable to shake him off, she lifted her blouse to reveal cancerous breasts. Llull retired in isolation to Puig de Randa to ponder a life of youthful excess. These days pilgrims to Puig de Randa are as likely to be weekend cyclists in search of a challenge as seekers after religious truth.

The winding road to the summit leads to three separate hermitages. The lowest, Oratori de Nostra Senyora de Gràcia, is perched on a ledge in the cliff above a sheer 200m (655ft) drop. Further up is the Santuari de Sant Honorat and finally Santuari de Cura, where Llull lived. The sense of history is somewhat offset by the radio mast on the mountain top and the electric candles in the church, but this is still a special place. Visit the Sala Gramàtica to see Llull's original manuscripts and a bottle of 1934 Chartreuse

made in the monastery, then look out from the terrace at the views of the plain, with Palma Bay and the isle of Cabrera in the distance. Modest, pleasantly renovated rooms (all en-suite) are available.

✚ 19J ☎ 971 120260 🖐 Free 🍴 Restaurant at Santuari de Cura (€€)

SANTA EUGÈNIA

People argue over whether the mountains or the coast represent 'the real Mallorca', but the heart of the island is to be found in villages like this, surrounded by farmland with views to where the mountains rise out of the plain. The 6km (4-mile) cart track to the neighbouring village of Sencelles offers good walking, and there is also the climb to Puig de Santa Eugènia. Natura Parc (➤ 70–71), on the edge of the village, is a popular family attraction with nature trails and indigenous farm animals, as well as a butterfly garden.

✚ 5E 🍴 Local bars (€) 🚌 One or two buses daily from Palma ❓ Market held Sat

SANTA MARÍA DEL CAMÍ

This market town on the Palma–Inca railway has developed a reputation as one of Mallorca's artistic centres. Most of the island's potters work close by, in Pòrtol (➤ 175), and Santa María is the centre of manufacture of *roba de llengues* ('cloth of tongues'), cotton woven into bright zigzag patterns and used in curtains, bedspreads and upholstery. Just off the main square is Ca'n Conrado, former Carmelite cloisters and a peaceful retreat from the traffic on the Palma road.

✚ 5E 🍴 Bars and cafés (€) 🚋 From Palma and Inca ❓ Market held Sun

SANTANYÍ

Do not be surprised if the buildings in Santanyí look just that little
bit more mellow than everywhere else – this small town is the
source of the golden sandstone used in Palma's cathedral and La
Llotja, among others. The old gate, Sa Porta Murada, seen as you

enter the town
from Palma, is a
good example of
Santanyí stone
and a reminder
that this was
once a walled
town. The parish
church of Sant
Andreu Apòstel
contains a
massive rococo
organ, designed
by Jordi Bosch

and brought here from a convent in Palma. The streets around the
church are the focus for one of Mallorca's liveliest markets.

✠ 2L1 ⑪ Bars and cafés (€) 🚌 From Palma and Cala Figuera ❓ Market
held Wed, Sat; Sant Andreu *festa*, 30 Nov

SANTUARI DE SANT SALVADOR

This old hermitage, 509m (1,670ft) above sea level at the highest
point of the Serra de Llevant, was the senior house of Mallorca's
monastic order and the last to lose its monks, in 1992. It is still a
popular place of pilgrimage, flanked by two enormous landmarks –
to one side a 14m (46ft) stone cross, to the other a 35m (115ft)
column topped by a statue of Christ holding out his right hand in
blessing. The church contains a fine carved alabaster retable, but
more interesting is the side chapel off the gatehouse, full of
poignant mementos and prayers to Our Lady. Like other former

monasteries, Sant Salvador has a few simple rooms available for pilgrims.

The views from the terrace take in Cabrera, Cap de Formentor and several other hilltop sanctuaries dotted across the plain. From the statue of Christ you look out towards the Castell de Santueri, a 14th-century rock castle built into the cliffs on the site of a ruined Arab fortress.

✠ 22J ✉ Signposted from Felanitx–Porto Colom road ☎ 971 827282 🅿 Free
🍴 Bar-restaurant (€) and picnic tables

SES COVETES

The name of this village means 'small caves' and this is believed to refer to Roman burial chambers on the same site. Nowadays people come here for one thing – to get to Platja Es Trenc, a 3km (2-mile) stretch of fine white sand backed by gentle dunes. This has long been an unofficial nudist beach, even during the puritanical Franco era. A little of the hippy atmosphere is retained around the *chiringuitos* (beach bars), and the beach certainly makes a peaceful, less commercial contrast to some of the other resorts on this coast.

✠ 20L 🚌 From Palma, Jul–Aug, three times a day

SES SALINES

This small town between Santanyí and Colònia de Sant Jordi is named after the nearby saltpans, which act as a magnet for migrant waders and wildfowl on their way from Africa to their breeding grounds in Europe each spring. Cap de Ses Salines, Mallorca's southernmost point, is another good spot for birdwatching. The town itself makes a pleasant place to stroll, with an abundance of local Santanyí sandstone which turns golden in the sun.

Just outside Ses Salines, on the road to Santanyí, is **Botanicactus,** one of Europe's largest botanical gardens, with bamboo and palm trees and, extraordinarily diverse in form, dozens of varieties of cactus.

➕ 21L 🍴 Bars and cafés (€) 🚌 Between Colònia de Sant Jordi and Santanyí ❓ Market held Thu

Botanicactus

✉ Carretera Ses Salines– Santanyí, km1 ☎ 971 649494; www.botanicactus.com 🕓 May–Sep daily 9–7; Jan–Apr, Oct daily 9–5.30; Nov–Dec daily 10:30–4:30 💷 Expensive

SINEU

Sineu, at the geographical centre of Mallorca, comes alive each Wednesday morning at the island's most traditional market. It takes place on several levels. The sound of bleating leads you to the livestock market, where weather-beaten farmers haggle over the price of sheep before heading for the town's *celler* restaurants for an early brunch. Further up, on the way to the church, you pass the symbol of Sineu, a winged lion; near here are numerous stalls selling leather, lace and pearls. Eventually you reach Sa Plaça, the church square, where the action is liveliest of all, as local housewives turn out to buy the week's food. Buckets of olives, strings of tomatoes, bags of squirming snails – they are all here, along with plenty of fresh fruit, vegetables and flowers. Get to Sineu early, before the tour buses arrive, to catch the flavour of a traditional country market. Good buys include dried figs and apricots, pottery from Pòrtol and baskets from Sudan. Also in Sineu is **S'Estació,** an unusual modern art gallery based in the old station.

✚ 7E 🍴 Several restaurants (€€) 🚌 From Palma ❓ Market held Wed

S'Estació

✉ Carrer Estació 2 ☎ 971 520750 🕐 Mon–Fri 9:30–1:30, 4–7, Sat 9:30–1 ✋ Free

VILAFRANCA DE BONANY

As you drive through this small town on the old road from Palma to Manacor, you cannot help noticing the strings of vegetables hanging outside several of the shops – peppers, aubergines, garlic and, above all, tomatoes. These are the famous *tomàtigues de ramallet*, sold on their stalks to be spread over *pa amb oli*. Vilafranca is also known for its honeydew melons, whose harvest is celebrated with a large melon festival each September. The other reason for coming here,

apart from food, is to visit **Els Calderers,** a manor house between Vilafranca and Sant Joan. This was once at the centre of a great wine estate, but like so many others it fell victim to the phylloxera disease. Reopened in 1993, the 18th-century house is now a museum of Mallorcan furniture and traditions; you can visit the wine cellar, granary, bakery, chapel and wash house, as well as wander around the main house with its paintings, guns and hunting trophies.

✚ 21H 🚍 From Palma and Manacor ❓ Market held Wed

Els Calderers

✉ Carretera Palma–Manacor, km37 ☎ 971 526069 🕐 Apr–Sep daily 10–6; Oct–Mar daily 10–5 💰 Expensive 🍴 Café (€)

HOTELS

ALGAIDA
Raims (€€)
Rural apartments around the courtyard of a 17th-century manor house. Breakfast is taken in a delightful garden of palm trees.
✉ Carrer Ribera 21 ☎ 971 665157; www.finca-raims.com

CALA FIGUERA
Villa Serena (€)
Simple two-star hotel, at the mouth of a pretty bay.
✉ Carrer Virgen del Carmen 37 ☎ 971 645303 🕓 Apr–Oct

MANACOR
La Reserva Rotana (€€€)
See page 68.

SANTA MARÍA DEL CAMÍ
Read's (€€€)
Stunning, British-run converted *finca*, set in lavish gardens with a palm-fringed pool. Boasts a Michelin-starred restaurant (➤ 185) and an excellent bistro.
✉ Carretera Santa María–Alaró ☎ 971 140261; www.readshotel.com

SINEU
Son Cleda (€€€)
Attractive three-star hotel in a restored 17th-century house overlooking the market square.
✉ Plaça Es Fossar 7, Sineu ☎ 971 521040

RESTAURANTS

ALGAIDA
Cal Dimoni (€€)
Meat and blood sausages grilled over an open fire at the 'house of the devil'.
✉ Carretera Palma–Manacor, km21 ☎ 971 665035 🕓 Noon–midnight; closed Wed

Ca'n Mateu (€€)

Roast sucking pig and other specialities beside a pool and children's play area.

✉ Carretera Palma–Manacor, km21 ☎ 971 665036 🕐 Lunch, dinner; closed Tue

BINISSALEM
Scott's Bistro (€€)

Cosy, candlelit atmosphere and a menu of freshly prepared market cuisine – steaks, fish, vegetables.

✉ Carrer Pou Bo 20 ☎ 971 870076 🕐 Mon–Sat 7pm–midnight

INCA
Celler Ca'n Ripoli (€€)

Founded in 1782, with dark wooden beams, chandeliers and wine vats around the walls. Mallorcan cuisine.

✉ Carrer Jaume Armengol 4 ☎ 971 500024 🕐 Lunch, dinner; closed Sun

Celler Son Aloy (€€)

Rustic grill and wine-tasting cellar in the middle of Mallorca's biggest vineyard, just outside Inca.

✉ Carretera Inca–Sencelles km3 ☎ 971 502302 🕐 Lunch Tue–Sun, dinner Wed–Sat

MONTUÏRI
Puig de Sant Miquel (€€)

See page 60.

PETRA
Sa Plaça (€€)

Prawns with chocolate sauce is just one of the old-style Mallorcan dishes at this small hotel-restaurant on the main square.

✉ Plaça Ramón Llull 4 ☎ 971 561646 🕐 Lunch, dinner; closed Tue

PORRERES
Centro (€)

See page 60.

PORTO COLOM
Colón (€€€)
One of the top restaurants on the island, with a terrace overlooking the fishing port. Modern Mediterranean cuisine.
✉ Carrer Cristobal Colón 7 ☎ 971 824783 ⏰ Lunch, dinner; closed Wed

SANTA EUGÈNIA
L'Escargot (€€)
French classics and a menu that changes regularly. Also pancakes, cheeses and French and Spanish *tapas*.
✉ Carrer Major 48 ☎ 971 144535 ⏰ Dinner Wed–Sat, Sun lunch

SANTA MARIA DEL CAMÍ
Ca'n Calet (€€)
Bustling restaurant just off the main road in an old town house with a pretty garden. Good value Spanish/Mallorcan food.
✉ Plaça dels Hostals 26 ☎ 971 620173 ⏰ Lunch, dinner daily

Read's (€€€)
British chef Marc Fosh conjures up sublime creations such as grilled sea-bass in liquorice sauce at this grand country hotel, one of the top culinary experiences on Mallorca.
✉ Carretera Santa Maria-Alaró ☎ 971 140261 ⏰ Lunch, dinner daily

Simply Fosh (€€)
See page 61.

SINEU
Celler Sa Font (€€)
Traditional *celler* – very busy on market day (Wed).
✉ Plaça d'Espanya 18 ☎ 971 520313 ⏰ Lunch, dinner daily

SHOPPING
ARTS AND CRAFTS
Ca's Canonge
Great for pottery, especially heavy brown-glazed cooking pots.
✉ Carrer Ca's Canonge 41, Pòrtol ☎ 971 602361

Ca Madò Bet
The lovely handmade and painted *siurells* (➤ 175) are made here.
✉ Carrer Jaume I 10, Sa Cabaneta, Pòrtol ☎ 971 602156

Camalu
One of the finest leatherware stores in eastern Mallorca, with elegant bags and hand-made boots and shoes.
✉ Carrer Ariel 28, Cala d'Or ☎ 971 642075

Ceramiques de Santanyí
Innovative ceramic designs based on ancient Mallorcan traditions.
✉ Carrer Guardia Civil 22, Santanyí ☎ 971 163128

Majórica
Shop here after touring Mallorca's largest pearl factory (➤ 168).
✉ Avinguda Majórica 48, Manacor ☎ 971 550200

OlivArt
Emporium where everything is made from olive wood.
✉ Carretera Palma–Manacor, km45, Manacor ☎ 971 552800

Roca Llisa
One of the best places to buy *siurells* (➤ 175).
✉ Carrer Roca Llisa 24, Pòrtol ☎ 971 602497

ENTERTAINMENT

DISCO
Riu Palace
Huge club playing European dance and chart hits, though there's also a Soul Session with funk and R 'n' B.
✉ Las Maravillas, Platja de Palma ☎ 971 743474; www.riupalace.com
🕒 11pm–6am; nightly in summer

GOLF COURSE
Son Antem Este
See page 72.

Sight Locator Index

This index relates to the maps on the covers. We have given map references to the main sights of interest in the book. Grid references in italics indicate sights featured on the town plans. Some sights within towns may not be plotted on the maps.

Index

Acknowledgements

The Automobile Association would like to thank the following photographers and companies for their assistance in the preparation of this book.

Abbreviations for the picture credits are as follows – (t) top; (b) bottom; (c) centre; (l) left; (r) right; (AA) AA World Travel Library

4bl Cala Figuera, AA/P Baker; **4bc** Tram, Soller, AA/P Baker; **4br** Deia, AA/P Baker; **5bl** Restaurant, Valldemossa, AA/C Sawyer; **5br** Palma, AA/P Baker; **6/7** Cala Figuera, AA/P Baker; **8/9** Placa Major, Palma, AA/J Cowham; **10bl** Cathedral, Palma, AA/K Paterson; **10/11t** Cap De Formentor, AA/P Baker; **11cl** San Vincente, AA/K Paterson; **11bl** Cala Pi, AA/K Paterson; **12bl** AA/K Paterson; **12br** Port of Soller, AA/C Sawyer; **13t** Market, Palma, AA/P Baker; **13c** AA/C Sawyer; **14/15t** Santa Maria Del Cami, AA/K Paterson; **14b** Palma, AA/C Sawyer; **15t** AA/K Paterson; **16b** Cala Figuera, AA/K Paterson; **16/17** Palau March Museum, Palma, AA/C Sawyer; **17t** Gorg Blau reservoir, Serra de Tramuntana, AA/K Paterson; **17b** Pollenca, AA/C Sawyer; **18** Reial Cartoixa, Valldemossa, AA/K Paterson; **19** Cala Guya, AA/K Paterson; **20/21** Tram, Soller, AA/P Baker; **25** Traditional dancing, AA/K Paterson; **27** Harbour at Palma, AA/C Sawyer; **28/29b** Road near Orient, AA/C Sawyer; **30** Policeman on bicycle, AA/C Sawyer; **34/35** Deia, AA/P Baker; **36tl** Portal del Moll, AA/J Cowham; **36/37** Roman remains, Pollentia, AA/C Sawyer; **37br** Portal Del Moll, AA/C Sawyer; **38/39t** Portals Vells, AA/K Paterson; **38/39b** Magaluf, AA/K Paterson; **40** Cap de Formentor, AA/P Baker; **41** Cap de Formentor, AA/P Baker; **42/43t** Castell d'Alaro, AA/P Baker; **42b** Castell d'Alaro, AA/K Paterson; **44/45b** Coves d'Arta, AA/K Paterson; **45t** Coves d'Arta, AA/P Baker; **46/47t & 46/46b** Deia, AA/K Paterson; **46bl** Deia, AA/W Voysey; **48/49** View from Es Baluard. © imagebroker/Alamy; **49** View through stone archway to art museum. © George Spark/Alamy; **50cl** Chapel Dome, Lluc, AA/K Paterson; **50/51b** Monastery, Lluc, AA/C Sawyer; **51tl** Statue of the Virgin, Lluc, AA/K Paterson; **52cl, 52/53 & 53br** Palma Cathedral, AA/K Paterson; **54b & 54/55t** Valldemossa, AA/K Paterson; **55cl** Portrait of George Sand, monastery at Valldemossa, AA/P Baker; **56/57** Valldemossa, AA/C Sawyer; **58 & 58/59** Shopping, AA/C Sawyer; **60/61** Pollenca, AA/C Sawyer; **62/63** Puig de Randa, AA/P Baker; **64** Marina, Santa Ponca, AA/W Voysey; **65** Porto Cristo, AA/K Paterson; **66/67** Es Trenc, AA/K Paterson; **69** Scott's Hotel, Binissalem, AA/C Sawyer; **70/71** Aquacity, S'Arenal, AA/K Paterson; **73** Golf near Llucmajor, AA/C Sawyer; **74** Palma, AA/K Paterson; **76/77 & 83** La Rambla, Palma, AA/K Paterson; **79** Ceramic plates, AA/K Paterson; **80/81** Palma, AA/P Baker; **84** Arab Baths, Palma, AA/P Baker; **85** Statue of Junipero Serra, Basilica de Sant Francesc, AA/P Baker; **86** Fundacio La Caixa, AA/K Paterson; **87** Fundacio Pilar I Joan Miro, AA/P Baker; **88t** Can Corbella, AA/C Sawyer; **88/89b** Placa Cort, AA/K Paterson; **89br** Statue of Jaume I of Aragon, Placa d'Espanya, AA/K Paterson; **90** Olives for sale, AA/M Jourdan; **91** Museu D'Art Espanyol Contemporani, AA/K Paterson; **92tr** Museu de Mallorca, AA/K Paterson; **92cl** Palau de L'Almudaina, AA/K Paterson; **93** Palau de L'Almudaina, AA/P Baker; **94/95** Palau March, AA/C Sawyer; **95br** Passeig des Born, AA/P Baker; **96** Poble Espanyol, AA/P Baker; **105** Puigpunyent, AA/K Paterson; **106/107t** Andratx, AA/P Baker; **107br** Banyalbufar, AA/P Baker; **108bl** Potter in La Granja, AA/K Paterson; **108/109** Watchtower close to Estellencs, AA/P Baker; **109tr** Coastline near Estellencs, AA/K Paterson; **110** Mural depicting Calvia's history, AA/K Paterson; **111** Galilea, AA/K Paterson; **112 & 113** La Granja, AA/K Paterson; **114/115t** Magaluf, AA/K Paterson; **114/115b** Palma Nova, AA/J Cowham; **116** Port d'Antratx, AA/K Paterson; **116/117b** Portals Vells, AA/K Paterson; **118** La Reserva, AA/K Paterson; **119t & 119b** View towards Sa Dragonera, AA/K Paterson; **120** Relief depicting landing of Jaume I in 1229, Santa Ponca, AA/W Voysey; **123** Cala de Sant Vicenc resort, AA/J Cowham; **124/125** Cala de Sant Vicenc, AA/P Baker; **126tl** Fornalutx, AA/P Baker; **126/127** Jardins de Alfabia, AA/K Paterson; **128** Orient, AA/C Sawyer; **128/129b** Placa Major, Pollenca, AA/K Paterson; **130t** Port de Pollenca, AA/P Baker; **130b** Port de Soller, AA/P Baker; **131** Sa Calobra, AA/P Baker; **132** Gorg Blau reservoir, AA/K Paterson; **134t** Church of Sant Bartomeu, Soller, AA/K Paterson; **134b** Banco Central Hispano, Soller, AA/K Paterson; **135** Soller, AA/K Paterson; **136** Son Marroig, AA/K Paterson; **143** Arta, AA/K Paterson; **144/145t** Arta, AA/P Baker; **145c** Madonna with Child, Santuari de St Salvador, Arta, AA/K Paterson; **146t** Cala Millor, AA/P Baker; **146c** Cala Rajada, AA/K Paterson; **147** Capdepera, AA/K Paterson; **148** Sant Joan Baptista, AA/P Baker; **149** Museu Etnologic de Mallorca, AA/K Paterson; **150b** Track to Puig de Maria, AA/J Cowham; **150/151t** Punta de n'Amer, AA/P Baker; **152t & 152c** S'Albufera, AA/C Sawyer; **153** Ses Paisses, AA/J Cowham; **158t & 158c** Ca'n Gordiola glass factory, Algaida, AA/K Paterson; **159** Cabrera, AA/C Sawyer; **160/161b** Cala Figuera, AA/K Paterson; **161cr** Campos, AA/P Baker; **162/163t** Capocorb Vell, AA/K Paterson; **163b** Colonia de Sant Jordi, AA/P Baker; **165** Coves del Drac, AA/K Paterson; **166t** Ermita de Bonany, AA/P Baker; **166b** Sant Miquel, Felanitx, AA/K Paterson; **167** Leather factory, Inca, AA/P Baker; **168/169** Placa d'Espanya, Llucmajor, AA/K Paterson; **169br** Pearl factory, Manacor, AA/K Paterson; **170bl** Birthplace of Fray Junipero Serra, Petra, AA/J Cowham; **170br** Portrait of Fray Junipero Serra, AA/P Baker; **171** Platja de Palma, AA/P Baker; **172/173** Sant Miguel, Felanitx, AA/K Paterson; **172b** Porreres, AA/K Paterson; **174/175t** Porto Colom, AA/K Paterson; **175** Porto Cristo, AA/K Paterson; **176b** Puig de Randa, AA/P Baker; **176/177t** Hermitage, Puig de Randa, AA/K Paterson; **178** Santanyi, AA/P Baker; **178/179** Column at Santuari de Sant Salvador, AA/P Baker; **180** Botanicactus, Ses Salines, AA/K Paterson; **181** Sineu, AA/K Paterson; **182** Vilafranca de Bonany, AA/K Paterson.

Every effort has been made to trace the copyright holders, and we apologise in advance for any accidental errors. We would be happy to apply the corrections in the following edition of this publication.

Dear Reader

Your comments, opinions and recommendations are very important to us. Please help us to improve our travel guides by taking a few minutes to complete this simple questionnaire.

You do not need a stamp (unless posted outside the UK). If you do not want to cut this page from your guide, then photocopy it or write your answers on a plain sheet of paper.

Send to: **The Editor, AA World Travel Guides, FREEPOST SCE 4598, Basingstoke RG21 4GY.**

Your recommendations...

We always encourage readers' recommendations for restaurants, nightlife or shopping – if your recommendation is used in the next edition of the guide, we will send you a **FREE AA Guide** of your choice from this series. Please state below the establishment name, location and your reasons for recommending it.

_____
_____
_____
_____
_____

Please send me **AA Guide** _____

About this guide...

Which title did you buy?

AA _____

Where did you buy it? _____

When? <u>m m</u> / <u>y y</u>

Why did you choose this guide? _____
_____
_____
_____
_____

Did this guide meet your expectations?

Exceeded ☐   Met all ☐   Met most ☐   Fell below ☐

Were there any aspects of this guide that you particularly liked? _____
_____
_____
_____

continued on next page...

Is there anything we could have done better? _____

_____

_____

About you...

Name (Mr/Mrs/Ms) _____

Address _____

_____

_____ Postcode _____

Daytime tel nos _____

Email _____

Please only give us your mobile phone number or email if you wish to hear from us about other products and services from the AA and partners by text or mms, or email.

Which age group are you in?
Under 25 ☐   25–34 ☐   35–44 ☐   45–54 ☐   55–64 ☐   65+ ☐

How many trips do you make a year?
Less than one ☐   One ☐   Two ☐   Three or more ☐

Are you an AA member? Yes ☐   No ☐

About your trip...

When did you book? m m / y y   When did you travel? m m / y y

How long did you stay? _____

Was it for business or leisure? _____

Did you buy any other travel guides for your trip? _____

If yes, which ones? _____

_____

_____

Thank you for taking the time to complete this questionnaire. Please send it to us as soon as possible, and remember, you do not need a stamp (unless posted outside the UK).

AA Travel Insurance call 0800 072 4168 or visit www.theAA.com